Uncommon Value

A rare book dealer's world

Francis J. Manasek

Arbor Libri Press
Ann Arbor, Michigan
1995

First edition 1995

ISBN №1-883817-02-1

Francis J. Manasek
G.B. Manasek, Inc.
Box 1204
Norwich VT 05055 USA
Tel: 802 649 1722
Fax: 802 649 2256

Introduction

Being an antiquary is an intensely personal activity and we all approach the business in our individual ways. This book is an anecdotal narrative of my own travels through the world of the collector and dealer and my personal observation, impressions, and analyses of the world that surrounds, supports, and nourishes both collectors and dealers. It deals with some very technical aspects of this world as well as human events: events venal and events noble. Many of the situations are universal and if you think you can identify all the people involved in them, you are wrong. Many have been distorted deliberately beyond sensible recognition. This book is not a kiss-and-tell. Rather, it is an attempt to analyze, and put into a human context, some of the things that can happen to those of us fortunate enough to be in this wonderful business, buying and selling bits and pieces of ages past.

Written with an appreciation for all the people and places I have known; the good times, the excitement and the laughter, I share it with my fellow dealers, my wonderful clients, and all those other people who poke around in odd places, looking.

We all share in the search for the special item, the search for the perfect venue and, most important, the search for ourselves; our own Philosopher's Stone, our own Grail.

Based on my experience, I can assure you that what you seek is just on the next shelf. But if you really believe this, then you won't know when you've found it.

Contents

Chapter 1

Behind the covers

"Oh, you're so lucky. I've always wanted to run a used bookstore!"

These are the words that separate Us from Them. It doesn't matter if some of the Us really don't "run a used bookstore," we are perceived as doing so by the Them, and that is what matters.

Drive along the back roads of New England (in particular) and many of the towns through which you'll pass will boast a used bookshop. For some reason, little towns in the Midwest don't seem to have books, or at least don't like to admit to having them by the open advertisement of bookshops. It probably violates some populist ethic. When there are bookshops, they usually are something like "Hanson's Used Book and Bible Store." Books on either coast don't violate some dark egalitarian need and their sale is advertised openly. Not hidden away like some whorehouse of the mind. Often, these little shops proclaim boldly "Rare Books" or "Antiquarian Books Bought and Sold." It's quite easy to wile away a few pleasant hours browsing these "Ye Olde Booke Shoppes." Almost invariably you'll be met by pleasant people with a greater or lesser number of books on their shelves as well as a greater or lesser knowledge about books and bookselling. If you are a "reader" you quite likely could be rewarded pleasantly with a few, or with an armful of moderately priced good second-hand books. If you're a collector with a collecting interest in books much older than fifty years, you'll most likely be disappointed, hopefully pleasantly.

This is because most used bookshops are just that. They are shops wherein one can buy a nice reading copy of the *New York Times Cookbook,* or any number of preread mysteries. Some shops seem to specialize, and there might be concentrations of bird books, plant and flower books or, say, travel books. Usually we can find a section on Science and Medicine, one on Religion, another on Poetry, and possibly Exploration or History. Occult, or Curiosa sections used to be located in the far crepuscular reaches where furtive people groped and fondled their way along the shelves. Since the content of most of these books is now part of the normal third grader's knowledge, this section seems to have declined. I wonder where the skulkers go now?

I've always been intrigued by shelves marked "Foreign Language Books" and have always harbored the suspicion that this is where a book is placed when someone hasn't got God's own idea what language it's written in, let alone what it's about. Would a 16th century Aristotle with parallel Greek and Latin texts go under 'Foreign Language?" I cringe to think it would.

Many books in our Ye Olde Booke Shoppe will have library stamps in them. Boldly will the rubberstamp proclaim "Hartford Public Library" on the title page, front free-end paper, and the back of every plate in the book. There will also be white lettering on the spine (sometimes rubbed off, creating a whitish smear and scuffed spine) and the remnants of a card pocket on the inside back board. I say "board" instead of "cover" not only to be snotty, but, since we're going to be talking about books throughout this book, I might as well use the lingo. "Boards" refers to what is commonly called the "covers" as in hard-cover or soft-cover. They are called boards because they once were just that.

Uncommon Value

Usually covered with leather, but nonetheless two slabs of wood. End pages are the blank sheets of paper that one sees when one lifts the board (front cover is the top board; back cover is the bottom board). One blank sheet is usually pasted to the inside of the top board, there is another blank sheet forming the first "page" of the book; this is the "front free-end paper." Sometimes abbreviated ffep. The same holds true for the back of the book, except substitute the word "back (or bottom)" for "front."

The presence of library stamps in these books doesn't mean that they're hot. It generally means that they've been sold, or de-accessioned, by the library to make room for more books. Or, the library has gone out of business and has sold off its contents. From a collector's standpoint, such a book, known as ex-library, or XL, is not worth as much as one without such marks. "This shop is mostly ex-library" is a pejorative. At any rate, Ye Olde Booke Shoppe serves a great public service, buying and recycling old books.

Many times I have heard the observation that one no longer finds rare books, or true antiquarian books in such places. For the most part this is true. I don't mean bargains or "sleepers" which are books whose value is unknown to the proprietor. These, of course, still occur in all shops. None of us can know the market in all types of books and some sleepers will indeed slip through our fingers. But truly rare and antiquarian books are no longer found in neighborhood second-hand bookshops. They've all gone somewhere else.

This was not always the situation. I grew up in New York City. When I was a teenager in the 1950's, New York's fabled Fourth Avenue booksellers were still in full force. I would scout them almost weekly and find wonderful things that were affordable, even to me, a kid on an allowance! I built a very nice collection of polar exploration on that allowance, including works by Hall, Payer, Kane, Shackleton and many of the important Franklin expedition books. I also have a collection of astronomy and science books that I assembled from those shops, paid for with money from an allowance and odd jobs. I could not do that today. Even in the 60's, when I was a student in Boston, the bookshops still had great stuff. I remember, for example, some wonderful buys at the Starr Bookshop in the Lampoon building on Plympton Street in Cambridge. By great buys I don't mean that I got fantastically underpriced great works. I mean that I was able to find important books in a discipline, books that helped shape and form an aspect of human endeavor; books that would be considered germinal in a major way. Such books were available in these shops. The fact that I could afford them was simply prima facie evidence that they were underpriced.

Many of these shops are gone. Certainly the great Fourth Avenue sellers are gone, initially decimated by rising rents, then by age and changing markets. The shops that do remain no longer have the same great inventories possible thirty or forty years ago.

This is true all over the world. General antiquarian shops in the old sense no longer exist in any number. We can find specialist shops, dealers in, say, travel, who maintain a large inventory of antiquarian and rare books in this area, but they won't have science or philosophy. And vice versa.

The specialist dealer has largely taken over. Perhaps it costs too much to remain competitive in many areas at the same time. Great bookselling firms in London, such as Francis Edwards, have folded and although the name remains, the inventory does not. The capital cost of maintaining strength in several disciplines of collecting is enormous. Probably impossible, since the return on invested capital is not enough to attract major new investment. I think that as large auction houses have taken over many of the historical activities of the rare book dealer, the dealer has had to evolve into a highly specialized beast occupying a relatively small ecological niche, one not too attractive to the larger animals, the auction houses. This has resulted in a slide toward the specialist and often very small back-bedroom dealers, dealers whose capital is knowledge not dollars but who can convert the former into the latter with hard work.

Gresham's law, I believe, states that bad money replaces good money. Thus, when the United States stopped putting silver into its coins, the old silver coins disappeared rapidly from circulation, replaced by the new base metal "clad" coins. The same holds true for books. As "better" or more important books disappeared from the marketplace, lesser works filled the shops. Unlike circulating coins, whose value, if they are precious metal, is determined by larger market forces, books' values are determined in a very small marketplace. Individuals knowledgeable in a particular field determine the desirability of a particular work. They put their money where their mouth is, and desirability is translated directly into purchase. Thus, the "better" books are sought after and bought actively. This creates a true free market and prices will respond to the relationship between demand and supply. The markets in books, maps, manuscripts and antiques in general represent probably the best examples of free markets in existence today. There is virtually no government control and prices are determined entirely by supply and demand.

Demand in maps and books is determined by factors that might be unique to this market. In antique furniture, for example, much of the value is in age. If I had a chair from the 16th century, original in all respects, no replaced stringers, no new finish, no replaced joints, it would probably be staggeringly valuable regardless of its origin. Indeed, any piece of 16th century furniture might be valuable, even if it had extensive repairs and refinishing. Not true for books. With only a few exceptions, age is not a major determinant of value. Books must pass an intellectual test first. Are they important in their discipline? That is the paramount question. To a lesser extent this factor intrudes into the furniture market. Certainly, pieces of Chippendale that are excellent unrestored examples of the master's work move into that plane, but truly old pieces get a value of their own that is distinctly age-related.

Lust is wonderful. It is the essence of the sensations that tell us we are alive. In youth it has a large component of venery but with age lust becomes more complex and even more wonderful. It becomes lust for knowledge, for a place in human history; for a tangible artifact of that history. This lust is probably the *élan locomotif* of collectors. True collecting is not the same is miserliness or the simple accumulation of wealth. Rather, it is the pinnacle of sensation; the communion with the intellectual forces that shaped us and the guardianship of this legacy. But it is, nonetheless, lust. And so it brings out the best and worst; the human foibles that afflict and define us all.

I noted that books, to be important from a collector's standpoint, must be important in the overall context or history of their discipline. This doesn't mean that the discipline itself must be important from the vantage of today's culture. For example, there are books important in the history of homeopathy or astrology, even though these disciplines have no empirical or rational claim to importance by today's criteria. It's one of the wonderful aspects of collecting - and one that is hardest for a beginner to understand - that irrespective of age, an important work in demonology is as important as a Fludd, a Cook or a Newton and (possibly) no less so than an early Mickey Mouse.

These kinds of value judgments about a printed work are difficult to make unless one is very familiar with the discipline. In the present era of political correctness, where every idea is considered equal, such determinations are particularly difficult to make. Younger people do not like to, and perhaps no longer can, make these distinctions. I am particularly amazed when some people argue that all cultures are equally good. Cultures that couldn't provide for, or protect their people when circumstances changed, cultures that make individuals self-destruct are clearly not the equal of cultures that don't have these attributes. These same

Uncommon Value

people, who give credence to herbal cures and astrology and argue that empirical medicine is unnatural, cannot be expected to make judgments about intellectual values of a book or map. Especially if it is written in another language, represents another culture or way of thinking, requires some knowledge or doesn't have pictures. I think this is a reason why much of book collecting is changing so rapidly.

There are fewer individuals coming into book collecting than ever before. There is, I think, a big difference between collecting serious artifacts of a cultural or intellectual tradition and collecting the intellectually ephemeral. Many individuals collect things, but many of these people seem to collect artifacts of their own youth. Sports cards, children's books, 1950's toys and games. None of these have yet proven themselves in the arena of global culture. Let me argue, for example, that many Germans collect American westward travel and Indian captivity narratives. Institutions both here and abroad have extensive holdings in these areas. Clearly these are areas that have, over time, transcended their immediate and parochial interests. Our own culture and other cultures have put these into some global perspective and have ascribed to them a modicum of importance and, consequently, a monetary value. Same for major explorations, scientific works, historical treatises and works of art. The trouble is that such assessments require rigorous analysis and some rigorous mentation is required. Serious collecting is serious stuff and the markets are serious markets. Just who buys things, who collects, and how do they do this. Of what cloth is a collector cut, or a dealer, for that matter?

Many people have the idea that because books are nice things and that it is fun to read, a bookstore is largely a game. It is not. The amount of knowledge required is vast and the business is capital intensive. An inventory of, say two hundred books, each costing three hundred dollars requires some sixty thousand dollars. And two hundred books is a small inventory indeed. The same two hundred item inventory in maps could easily run twice that amount. And these are very small middle to low-end inventories. Double the size of the inventory and add a good dose of items in the over two thousand dollar range and the figure is up to several hundred thousand dollars just for stock. I recently asked George Ritzlin, the Chicago dealer who used to be an accountant, what he thought it would take to set up a decent map business. He figured it would take a few hundred thousand dollars, at least. When I speculated that this kept a lot of people out of the business, George observed that it didn't. But it kept a lot of people dealing part time.

I was once asked "What does it take to be a part time map or print dealer?"

"A hundred bucks and a razor blade."

A serious inventory can easily absorb half a million dollars and that doesn't include reserves needed to buy in items that might come along unexpectedly. Half a million equals a lot of books if you're selling five or ten dollar books, but if the price range is in the thousands, then the number of books isn't very large at all. There are many dealers who bring well over this value of material to exhibit at fairs. It is very deceiving to try to estimate the value of inventory or sales on the basis of physical size of the inventory.

Years ago when I dealt in lower priced items I rarely had things selling for more than about five hundred dollars. However, the economics of this type of dealing is not to my liking. In order to make enough money selling in this price range, one would need a physically large operation. I wanted to stay small and not hire a large staff to handle large quantities of books and maps and I also didn't want to have other hassles and responsibilities of a big walk-in shop. I had acquired, years ago, the delicious habit of spending part of each year abroad and really didn't want to be tied down to a shop. I think having an open general used bookstore is sort of like having a dairy herd - you really can't go away. I began to deal in more and more expensive items, gradually replacing the cheaper inventory. In that process I learned that these were really quite different businesses.

Selling ten dollar used books is not the same business as selling thousand dollar books; selling fifty dollar local interest old maps is not the same as selling multi-thousand dollar maps of serious interest to collectors worldwide. These are not just quantitative differences, there are qualitative differences between dealing in inexpensive items and valuable items. There is a difference in attitude, in affect and in scholarship or knowledge as well as in size of the check. I have done both businesses and I enjoy them both. Indeed, I still have a branch of my business that deals in inexpensive items, but it is set up to require very little of my time. My personal involvement and enjoyment is in the area of the rare and nearly-rare.

Chapter 2

Hanover shop

███████████████████████████

One of the curses of having an open shop, even if it's located on the second floor of an office building, is that it attracts masses of people with nothing better to do than "visit that nice old bookshop." If you read Helene Hanff's *84 Charing Cross Road,* you know what I mean. After the war, Hanff bought books from Marks & Co., London booksellers and engaged one of the people who worked there in excruciatingly cute correspondence. Tons of it. She occasionally sent him some tinned ham, so I guess it wasn't all bad, although the poor fellow had to put up with self-consciously cute prattle for years. I think he finally faked his death.

This perversion, wherein otherwise mostly decent and normal people just *know* that anyone who works in a bookstore will be fascinated by their anecdotal trivia, is pandemic. Indeed, Hanff's book became a long running Broadway production, doubtlessly infecting even more minds and giving them license to torment honest booksellers. Some of these people even have a mild interest in books (although rarely the purchase of books) so they doubtless enjoy exchanging fish stories. It's their entertainment, but probably also a form of therapy that establishes their sense of worth. No unwashed louts are we, why, "That looks like a book my grandmother had."

The kind of books and maps I sell are rarely bought on impulse, although there are enough exceptions to keep alive the fantasy that it's worthwhile trying to entice such buyers. People who want these things seek out us dealers, but it is nice to be somewhat accessible and a central location is good. Unfortunately, an accessible central location also draws the Hanff-ites as well. Most of us have developed ways of protecting ourselves from these people and we readily share these techniques with each other at book fairs and other gatherings of the clans. We all have our favorite techniques of triage.

Having an upscale appearance saves many problems. Ken Nebenzahl, one of the world's major map dealers had such a place. It really wasn't a shop, but a very substantial office on North Michigan Avenue in Chicago. Occupying the entire floor of an office building, it had its own elevator stop. Everything in it spoke of quality, establishment, antiquity, authority. I suppose one way to describe it would be to say it had 'class.' A wonderful place, but nonetheless somewhat daunting. I recall the first time I visited. "What the hell am I doing here?" I thought. Ken was kind and gracious, showed me wonderful things. We have since done a respectable amount of business together.

My Hanover shop had massive mahogany glass-doored bookcases, carpeted floor and some very expensive material displayed prominently. The theory was that if I looked expensive and daunting, only people with serious interests would come in. It seemed to work reasonably well. Quite often people would come to the door, peer in and then flee. Sort of like the invisible odor-shield of TV deodorant ads. Not for them. If they penetrated my invisible shield and I was busy, they would have to pass a second test. I would peer at them over the top rim of my glasses and in my most resonant and professorial of voices would say "Good

F.J. Manasek

Afternoon. May we be of assistance?" Most people who just wanted to get in out of the rain preferred the rain to my solicitous and pompous inquiries and fled in terror. Of course, there were the ones who put their wet parcels down on the plan chests, walked right in and announced "I just want to browse." "We are terribly sorry," would be my response, "This is not a browsing shop. We have no open inventory but I'd be glad to show you anything that you might like to examine. Is there something specific you're looking for?" That usually worked. Of course if it was a slow day or if I wasn't busy on the telephone I didn't have to discourage visitors. Fiona, my more gregarious associate, on the other hand, always welcomed visitors and would spend hours chatting them up. It created a very pleasant atmosphere for idle browsers, but I'm not sure it was a very profitable use of time.

Despite the barricades, we had our regulars. They were wonderful people who adopted us. The guy from Burlington who always brought me a freshly baked loaf of bread. He would come to Hanover to visit his niece about once a month, and would usually stop by and show me some item that he wanted to sell. He also was a steady customer for old leaves. Never a very big buyer, but he was knowledgeable, never a pest and very civilized — he knew when we were busy and didn't impose. We, of course, had regular serious clients to whom we provided serious maps and books. It was always a joy to work with them and watch their collections grow.

On the other side of the spectrum was the minister who came in and looked at maps whenever he was in town. He claimed to be a map collector, and indeed knew a bit about 19th century maps. An offensive sort, he told us how much each of our maps was overpriced. There was also something wrong with the condition of each one. If not condition, then price, mostly both.

One day, after a particular trying session, this member of the First Estate strode to the door and announced that our prices were all outrageous. At that, he walked out, turned around and asked Fiona if we gave a clerical discount.

"Frankly, we discount all clerics." was Fiona's smiling reply.

He never got it.

City folk are smart and we hicks aren't too bright, or at least we must appear somewhat dim. Some assume we wear hay for warmth and eat squirrels for breakfast. I used to get visitors to my Hanover shop who thought I was running Ye Olde Rummage Shoppe in East Overshoe and that they were going to take Uncle Jethroe for a walk around the block. Some gave up very readily when they saw our books behind glass and mahogany doors. Some got as far as asking "How much for the bird books?" and then beat a hasty and puzzled (and sometimes angry) retreat when told "Five hundred-fifty for the pair." Some visitors never got it at all and would keep asking prices long after it became clear to everyone (almost) that we were not selling Reader's Digest Condensed Books.

Most curious were the ones who were going to use their superior knowledge to fleece the local sheep. I took them on as personal challenges. I remember well the pair from Yonkers. They loomed large in the doorway, these two people, man and wife, banded together and scouring the countryside for 'deals' and 'bargains' but, most immediately, blocking the remnant of autumn light that radiated from Jimmy's barbershop across the hall.

"Come in." I smiled at them as they seemed to hesitate. Pausing for but a moment, they broke their hesitation and the two people flowed into our little office, absorbing volumes of our limited space.

"Can we be of assistance to you?"

"I'm Sheldon Green and this is the wife, Mrs. Green." Mrs. Green, I learned later was Astrid. Sheldon and Astrid (the wife) exchanged knowing glances and, turning to me, Sheldon told me that they were collectors looking for prints.

"What kind of prints?"

Oh, sort of anything." The studied casualness of the response plainly meant that they were not going to tell me what they wanted for fear that I would jack up the price on anything that was of interest. If I didn't know of their interest in an item, my prices would of course be ridiculously low. This they knew.

"We no longer have a lot of prints, mostly maps."

Can we look?"

"Sorry, but everything is in the plan chests and we don't let people look through them - everything gets worn, you know."

Sheldon smiled conspiratorially. We were knowledgeable guys talking each other's language. "Anything, er, Japanese?"

Sorry, only a few Chikanobus and some Meiji period Haronobu reprints. Nothing very good."

What's in that drawer?"

"Maps."

"Oh. And in that one?"

"Some miscellaneous stuff we have left over. We used to deal a lot in prints, but now we mostly do maps. I think we have some Hogarth in here." Again that look. Sheldon and Astrid assumed very casual poses.

"We collect Hogarth. We might be interested in what you've got. If the price is right, of course."

"Of course." I opened the drawer. Sheldon ran his tongue over his lips. Astrid pushed closer. There was no room for me."Would you like to see any of these?"

"Sure."

I took out a stack of large folio prints. These were black and white engravings from some of the many Craddock editions of Hogarth's works. The original copper engraved plates to these impressions had been obtained, in the early 19th Century, from Hogarth's widow who was poverty-stricken after his death. After being reworked by Heath, they were reprinted many times and large folio volumes were published until well into the 19th Century. These were huge books, difficult to lift and difficult to keep anywhere in a library, let alone on a library shelf. Many of these books simply fell apart because of the great weight put upon the bindings which were stressed additionally by the awkward size of the volume. The paper was also one of those abominable early 19th C machine-made papers that had all the strength of a blotter and which foxed and darkened like crazy. All in all, one of the great triumphs of Victorian bookmaking. These books suffer one of two fates. Either they come apart spontaneously or their coming apart is dealer-assisted. The plates are splendid - not an acquired taste but one that requires the pre-existence of a degree of weirdness in the beholder. Strange images of babies being killed; animals tortured, the Idle 'Prentice who, after a short lifetime of waste and idleness is executed while his industrious peer marries the boss's daughter. Obese people boarding carriages; mockery of judicial wigs, a cock fight, mocking the clergy of France and numerous other well drafted politically incorrect insults to one group or another. Yet entirely wacko, sort of like an early Smokey Stover cartoon with every participant a bit bonkers. Interesting plates. And Sheldon and Astrid collected them.

We had several complete sets. The Idle 'Prentice (Industry and Idleness), Times of Day, Harlot's Progress, and several others. Sheldon and Astrid lusted. In his finest casual manner, Sheldon asked "How much for these old prints?"

"They are each marked."

They were priced fairly, yet robustly. The prices reflected New York markets more than local ones. Sheldon began to bargain.

F.J. Manasek

"How much if I take these three and that one? The prices are very high. I never pay this much. Where do you get these prints? How come they're so expensive?"

Finally Sheldon calmed himself. "Would you take.." and he named a figure "...for these?"

"Sheldon, I can't do that, but if you take this group of five in addition, then I'll make it so much." I countered with what seemed to be a generously discounted price. Clearly I was weakening, uncertain of myself.

"I know what these things are worth. I'm a collector." Sheldon was trying his best. Astrid was nodding agreement.

"Sheldon, tell you what. You tell me what prints you want and what you want to pay. You know a lot about these things. Let's work a deal."

Sheldon rose, victorious, to his full height and enjoyed the luxury of a quick knowing exchange with Astrid. He dove into the open plan chest drawer and, rooting about, pulled out several more sets and single Hogarth prints. He studied the marked prices carefully and finally made his offer.

"Sheldon, you got it!" I was clearly bested.

I rolled up the prints as Sheldon peeled off travelers' checks. We exchanged the roll of prints for the roll of checks and Sheldon and Astrid edged toward the door, lest I discover the folly of my ways and try to get my goods back.

"I know prices," said Sheldon as he and Astrid crossed the threshold.

"Yes indeed, you're just too much for a country dealer like myself."

Gloating Sheldon turned to me. As he did so, he noted the second brass plate on my door, the one listing the address of my London gallery. He paused a moment, reading, and lip-synching.

Uncommon Value

His expression changed and it was clear that, suddenly, Sheldon knew.

Every once in a great while someone would come in, spend a bit of time talking with either Fiona or me, ask a few seeming casual questions about an item on the wall, often a very expensive map, and say simply, I'll take it. This is the kind of purchase that sunshines an otherwise ordinary day. Selling a five thousand dollar map to someone you've never seen before, and likely will never see again, doesn't happen often enough. Here in New England impulse purchases seem to be largely the under hundred dollar variety. In Boston they're a bit more and in New York a few thousand dollars is not an uncommon impulse buy. But people who live here, where the ghosts of the Puritans still lurk in the lee of the conscious, don't do that. Some of the wildest spenders are Californians. Not Texans, in my experience, despite some wonderful legends within the trade.

A few years ago I was exhibiting at the San Francisco fair occupying the same space I'd had for years, sort of under a staircase near the middle of the huge exhibit. I liked that space, it wasn't the best in the fair but my clients knew where I was and could find me easily. Also, my neighbors were two of the most delightful booksellers I know, Ellen and Jim Herring of Trophy Room Books.

Among the books I had on display was a particularly nice copy of Agricola's *De re Metallica* that wonderful compendium of Medieval mining and metallurgy. It was about the nicest copy I'd seen, fine period binding, wide margins, clean paper. Midway through the fair there had still been no interest in the book when a passerby stopped, looking in the glass case, he pointed to the Agricola and asked me "How much?"

"Four thousand dollars."

"Is it a good book?"

"Oh, yes. Very."

"I'll take it, please." He handed me his American

F.J. Manasek

Express card, I ran up the sale, put the book in a bag and he was off. The whole transaction took less than five minutes.

Most of the sales from my Hanover space were to serious collectors who visited Hanover on business, holiday or, increasingly so, to call on me. I would attract the occasional Dartmouth College parent who was looking for "old Dartmouth books" or old College prints, none of which I ever had. Most of them were puzzled when I told them I didn't deal in that material. They assumed I depended upon the College for my trade. In reality, I don't think I ever had more than a half dozen serious clients who were part of the academic community. Some of my very best clients, however, were trustees, overseers and alumni.

Dartmouth College has some of the most loyal alumni of any college anywhere. There is a deeply felt attachment, kinship and gratitude to the College that is undiminished by time. Each year, at Homecoming, there is a long march through town of the returning alumni. The alumni are also most generous to their Alma Mater. I always enjoy being at book fairs in distant places and having the Old Greens come up to me to reminisce about their days in Hanover. Most of the time these encounters are very upbeat, with alumni of all ages making nicenoise about their Hanover days. Only once was I saddened by such a meeting. In Los Angeles, a middle aged alumnus approached me and asked for help in selling his collection of Dartmouth memorabilia. He had built a very extensive collection of items that went back into the 18th century, some from the early days just after the College's founding. Some would almost certainly be of interest to the College's own collection. I suggested that he might want to get his collection appraised and then make a gift of it the College. No, he decided, he really didn't want the College to have any of it, he had become disappointed and disillusioned with Dartmouth and just wanted to get rid of his collection and his memories. I didn't ask why, but his sadness was apparent. Certainly the Dartmouth of today is not the Dartmouth of his undergraduate days, but then neither is he nor the rest of the world. His collection has a very happy new home now, but I'll always wonder what caused his loss of faith.

My Father Christmas passed away
When I was barely seven.
At twenty-one, alack-a-day,
I lost my hope of heaven.
....
I don't know which loss hurt the worse-
My God or Santa Claus
Robert Service, The Sceptic

There has been a recent and lively correspondence in the British trade publications concerning NBB's (non-book-buyers) and how to spot them. The theory being that certain mannerisms, ways of dressing and speaking can be used to determine if someone coming into your shop is a buyer or a non-buyer. Comments such as "What a lovely shop!" or "I could spend hours in here." were noted as predictors of non-buyers.

To this list I add anyone who plays to the gallery. Richard M., whom I later learned was the scourge of local dealers, came into my shop when I first opened. He made a grand entry, waited until I saw him and then inhaled deeply. "Aaaah!" the connoisseur of bookish airs pronounced. "I love the smell of old books." He rubbed his hands together as if in anticipation and started looking around. I had just gotten in a Johnson's dictionary, the large first edition, and it was on a table waiting to be collated and catalogued. Richard strode over to it and with a practiced hand almost ripped off the top board. The price was penciled on the front fly leaf, I think it was around $4000.00. Richard snorted, muttered something inaudible and stalked out. Fortunately he never returned.

A few years later at the Los Angeles book fair I saw the same air-sampling performance, this time given by John LaRoquette, the actor. I hear he collects first editions.

Chapter 3

What is this worth?

The theory of value is complex, and I have to deal in a pragmatic universe. To me, and to most dealers, the possibility that there might be some absolute monetary value to something has no useful meaning in day to day existence. Something is worth how much you can get for it. And yet...

I occasionally find myself defining the value of money in terms of how much map it will buy. That's the reverse of defining the value of a map in terms of how much money is needed to get it, the more conventional and possibly the more sensible way to view the situation.

"How much is this worth?" is probably the most difficult question we get asked. 'Worth' has many possible meanings. It can mean replacement cost, what it will fetch at auction, what I will pay for it, what you will pay for it, what Uncle Sam will accept as a value if it is given to the local museum, what the insurance company will buy it for if the firemen have to hose it down, and so forth.

Mostly, when people come into my office with a book or map and ask that question, they are really asking either for replacement cost or what I will pay for it. If it is a common item then replacement cost isn't difficult to determine. I will (or should) know the prices of similar things currently on the market, or, at worst I would need a few telephone calls to find out. It's the scarcer stuff that can cause fits.

As an example, there is in my office, at the time I'm writing, a map that has a price of $12,000. listed in one of the (virtually useless) price guides. The map had been in a dealer's catalogue a few years ago and therefore this price found its way into the guide. A couple of years ago an exemplar changed hands privately for $40,000. and another last year for about $70,000. There probably aren't a dozen people who know of these transactions, but they affect profoundly the price of the map and make the public knowledge price listed in the guide worse than worthless. Just last week another copy sold at auction in London for £45,000. which translates, after exchange and buyer's premium, into something like $75,000. This price was realized because the bidders knew of the previous private transactions. The auction house did not, and had estimated the map at £10000. to £12000. So much for the specialized expertise of the auction houses! Aside from being a perfect lesson in the value of price guides and auction house estimates, this sequence of prices raises a real question. What should I charge for my copy of this map? Asked another way, what's it worth?

Reasonable. There might not be a more subjective word in the language or more subjective a concept in all peopledom. I personally learned the various perceptions of 'reasonable' when my first wife sued for divorce. I was told it would be 'reasonable' to give her anything she wanted. At the time I didn't think so, but did so anyway. Only later, after I escaped back home to New England with my son, did I realize just how reasonable that trade was. She had material possessions. I had my son. She still had the unnatural vicissitude of life in Chicago's Hyde Park. Jared and I had Vermont. I can think of no better sequence to illustrate the relativism of 'reasonable'.

Fortunately the concept of 'reasonable' when applied to transactions involving maps or books doesn't involve testosterone-laden divorce lawyers, or even a more gender neutral conflict. It means putting the item and the transaction into a broader context. This context must include, of course, previous transactions, but most also include the context of those transactions. It must include educated assessment of the importance of the item in the cultural history of the people who created it and the cultural history of the people who are selling it. Thailand controls the exportation of images of the Buddha. How many people in the United States would buy such an image of the Buddha? These kinds of cultural differences create local values. Many dealers, including myself, try to exploit these differences and buy where demand (i.e. the local culture has no use for) is low and sell where demand is higher.

Sometimes this confounds. I have my office in northern New England. People often assume that therefore I deal in New England maps and books. I get telephone calls and letters all the time both offering me items of local interest and seeking items of local interest. "No," I have to explain time and again "we do not have bird's eye views of New England towns; we do not have maps of Windsor, Vermont etc. etc." I recently got a brief note from someone in the state of Washington, asking that I no longer send him catalogues because "being a New England dealer, I understandably have local material and nothing relating to the Pacific Northwest." somewhat puzzled by this request, I looked into our last few catalogues. My memory was correct. About 20% of all the catalogued New World maps related to the Pacific Northwest.

In real estate, the three major determinants of price have been described as being "location, location and location." While not really true, we can make a similar emphasis in the map and book world and emphasize "condition, condition and condition." The value of a book or map is certainly, to some extent, related to its condition as well as other things. To be sure, a fine copy of the Gutenberg Bible can be exchanged for a lot of currency. But a tattered copy would do pretty well also. A single page could expect to realize about $9000; more if it's from a desirable (you figure this one out) part of the Bible. A really nice copy of Blaeu's America map, with original color might fetch $6000. whereas a derelict copy might fetch $2000. A great copy of Mitchell's 1865 United States map might reasonably sell for $60.00; a torn copy $5.00 on a good day to a not very knowledgeable buyer.

The examples I have listed are not meant to be mini price guides hidden within the text of this book, but rather examples to indicate that the concept of value is a complex one. Unless we understand the reasons why anyone collects something, who these collectors are and what place the collectable occupies in the cultural history of ourselves as a people we cannot understand value or prices.

Some years ago, beer cans became 'hot' in the collectables market. President Jimmy Carter's brother, Billy, had a beer named for him and Billy Beer cans, full or empty, fetched high prices. People bought, sold and traded beer cans. Flea markets had beer can 'specialists' many of whom had vans fitted with racks that were filled with cans. At the peak of 'beer-can-o-mania' some of these people had collections 'worth' tens of thousands of dollars. They are now 'worth' next to nothing. Why?

Beer, however wonderful a liquid, however thirst quenching on a hot day and however erudite one may wax on the national differences in beer quality, is but a relatively minor player in the élan vital of the culture of our race. Beer can collectors are beer drinkers and beer drinkers and beer can collectors do not, in the long run, determine lasting cultural values. After the novelty of collecting beer cans wore off, cans 'worth' hundreds of dollars were buyable for a buck or two. Baseball is a bit more ingrained and a more legitimate part of this culture. A significant number of well educated people follow baseball; an ex-president of Yale became Commissioner of Baseball (clearly a step up in intellectual circles). All this notwithstanding, baseball card collecting is but one notch above beer can collecting and may go flat at any time.

Modern first editions are the baseball cards of the literate set. As-new condition first edition books of popular (fashionable) dead authors may fetch thousands of dollars. If the dust jacket is present and in fine condition. If there is a tear in the dust jacket the book might be worth but a few hundred; if absent the book is worth a decent lunch. If one stands back and views it from a distance, as might an anthropologist, it doesn't make any sense. Modern firsts are a boom and bust business, one I stay away from. I firmly believe that there are general, more or less objective, importance ratings that can be ascribed to cultural artifacts. Spent brewskies are pretty low, baseball cards are pretty marginal. Modern firsts are iffy; some will become giants in our literary history but only with the blessings and acceptance by future generations; generations that are sufficiently far removed from today to have some greater, less immediate, perspective that dictates their decisions. Certainly a tear in the dust jacket has nothing to do with the cultural value of the contents and should be only a relatively minor factor in the value of the artifact. I shall continue to view modern firsts as cultural ephemera.

Pretty snotty, this decision making based on cultural values. That's a pretty foul arrogant ethnocentric bias. All cultures are equal, and I'm a white male, judgmental Eurocentric snob for making these observations. So be it. Every human artifact is a product of a culture; it is a cultural expression and as such must be judged against others from the same tradition and in the same context. Whether Eurocentric or not, some events of human history had a greater effect than others on subsequent human history. We can reshuffle priorities and to some extent have revisionist versions of the contributions to today's mainstreams made by different cultures and peoples, but the overall general flow of the river of history cannot be dammed or reversed or diverted.

Uncommon Value

Western physics, for example, is probably the best model of the physical universe there is or ever was. Put simply, it has heuristic value, and it works. We can predict the behavior of physical systems, measure the speed of light, release some energy from the atom, all exercises based upon the validity of our model. Many people may not like it, it might be difficult to comprehend, it might be threatening, but no other system of physics can do this. Prayer can't and reading chicken entrails can't. African tribes couldn't do it, Borneo farmers couldn't do it and Irish crofters couldn't do it. Whatever splendid achievements these various methodologies and groups may have accomplished, they didn't do a physics that works. Unfortunately in order to judge the importance of a contribution (or a non-contribution) to a field such as physics, we need to know something about the field. It's not a judgment that everyone can make, but however unfashionable it may be to be perceived elitist, we can all observe that all ideas are not equal and that the validity of a scientific model cannot be determined by plebiscite.

In dealing with the artifacts of science, the manuscripts, the publications and even the physical apparatus, we can let the marketplace determine importance. Guys who collect beer cans don't collect in the history of physics. And people who collect in the history of physics don't pay big bucks for the trivia. There are indeed seminal works that have contributed permanently to the intellectual gene pool of a discipline and these will always be sought after. The byways of collecting will always be paved with the intellectual discards. And this truth will ultimately sound the death knell to the fascists of political correctness. Let them remember (if they ever knew) the Lysenkoism once promulgated on the tips of bayonets and where it is now. Behold a work of Gregor Mendel and a work of Lysenko. You will know of what I speak.

Perhaps nowhere is the oft assumed dictum that 'older is more valuable' less valid than in the field of old maps. I have

F.J. Manasek

a stack of maps printed in the 16th century that I sell for between fifty and a hundred and fifty dollars each. These are genuine, authentic, guaranteed original maps. And there are some maps from the same period that fetch six figure prices. What accounts for this disparity? Antique furniture collectors might foam at the mouth if they could find any genuine, authentic, guaranteed original pieces of furniture from this era, especially in fine unrestored condition. There are two threads that run through map collecting. The decorative and the important. By applying some of the criteria I discussed above, we can establish a map's place in the history of cartography. Is it a breakthrough map in the history of the mapping of a particular area? Does it show, for the first time, a radically different or improved image? Is it linked to political events, essentially a cartopolitical statement of significance? These are the predominant questions that concern institutions, scholars and perhaps the more technical collectors. Many of these important maps are, to my eye, not very attractive at all. Some years ago I sold one of the rarest world maps, the so-called Florentine Goldsmith's map. This anonymous, rather small copperplate engraved map shows the world as known in the mid 1500's and is surrounded by an elaborate border. I don't recall how many copies of this map are known, but it is fewer than five. It is a puzzle in terms of where it fits into 16th century mapmaking. My copy of this map formed part of a wonderful cosmographical manuscript treatise. Written on paper, in Latin and Greek, with Hebrew notation, the manuscript was clearly contemporary to the map. In a fine, learned hand, the anonymous scholar who wrote the treatise had references to Copernicus, referring to him as any one of us might refer to the work of one of our contemporaries. Few collectors would be able to afford this map. I showed it to one of my clients who was developing a major map collection. His collection was evolving along lines of large, highly decorative and important maps and this little black and white item failed to elicit a second glance. Nonetheless, the Florentine Goldsmith's map was sold easily to another

Uncommon Value

collector and it occupies a major position in his internationally known collection. I am pleased that it has stayed together with the associated manuscript and perhaps some day the manuscript will shed some light on the origins of this elusive map. How my firm acquired this map makes a wonderful story. I'll have to write about it sometime. Condition, always an important determinant in the desirability of a map, hence its price, becomes less important with the really rare items. It's one thing to reject a map on the basis of condition if one can reasonably expect to find a better one in a few months or a year, but if there is no reasonable expectation of finding another one in the next twenty years, or perhaps ever, then condition pales and yields to scarcity.

I don't think one should ever buy a damaged map unless it's either very scarce or very cheap. In the present market a heavily damaged and repaired Blaeu Americas is not a bargain for $2000. A superb example for $6500. is. The little Florentine Goldsmith map was in only fair condition. Nonetheless scarcity prevailed. There was little likelihood that a private collector could ever obtain another. And yet, its price was undeniably lower than it could have been because of the condition problem.

Perhaps one of the most important services that a dealer can provide is placing a map or book not only in its cultural and historical perspective but in its condition hierarchy. Some maps, such as the relatively common *Carte Nouvelle de l'Amerique Angloise,* an attractive map of the American Colonies done by Conrad Lotter around 1770, and the 1750's Homann map of the New England colonies, *Nova Anglia Septentrionali Americæ* seem to appear most often with characteristic defects. In the case of these two maps, the most common defect is a pronounced age-darkening along the centerfold. This probably derives from the glue used to paste the binder's guard to the back, or verso, of the map. Binder's guards are strips of paper that were glued to maps so that when the map was assembled into an atlas the binder could sew through the guard and not have to put stitches through the map itself. I think the glues, most of which were animal glues, sometimes darkened excessively and discolored the underlying paper, something that seems to have happened also with many of the pretty maps done by Antonio Zatta in Venice in the latter 18th century. Some collectors don't mind the staining, but it is indeed possible to find these maps in virtually pristine condition. There might be a significant price premium, but in the long run it's worth it. This kind of knowledge about specific maps helps explain why there is often a relatively big price difference in catalogs, why a map may fetch a very high price at auction or not sell at all. Knowing things such as this about specific maps and passing this knowledge along to clients is a major service that knowledgeable dealers can provide since most collectors don't see the volume and diversity of maps that we dealers see. I find myself explaining this sort of thing quite often, especially when buying maps. Then I find it very helpful when I have another example in stock so that we can compare them, point by point. This is often useful when I have to explain to a seller why I am making what might seem to be a very low offer.

Many collectors, especially newer ones, seek out only colored maps. Every dealer has experienced the difficulty of selling an uncolored map, often taking only a fraction of what the item would fetch if it had been colored. Hence the occupation of colorist, people who earn their livelihood by coloring old maps and prints. It's a nice occupation if one enjoys solitary work. A colorist can live wherever he or she wants and if good, the world, or at least the UPS man, will indeed beat a path to the door. Colored maps are perceived to be more decorative than black and white ones. Prior to the 19th century and the invention of lithography, maps were printed either from wooden blocks or from engraved copperplates. The impressions were black, and color was not printed. In order to print colors, a different impression is needed for each color and this means that the sheet of paper with the image being built up on it by means of successive impressions must be aligned very carefully each time. Registration, as this alignment is called, is very difficult and the technical problems of registration precluded the commercial use of printing to produce colored images for a long time. Interestingly, in Japan the problem of registration was solved in the late 18th C, by, I believe, Haronobu, the great Ukiyo-e woodblock master. In the west it was not until the 19th century that printed color became common and commercially feasible. Instead, color was applied by hand, using watercolors, much the same way a child might color an outline image in a coloring-book. Or complete a paint-by-number scene. In reality only a very few colors were used and we can often recognize the colors and hues characteristic of particular mapmakers. For example, there are characteristic pinks, greens and yellows used by the Homanns in the early 1700's.

It was common for maps to be issued in different flavors. One could buy an uncolored, black and white map, or one could order it colored in outline only, or in full wash color, or even highlighted with gold leaf. All of these varieties are seen today in the market, but the gold highlighted ones are quite special. Often made for royalty, we usually see gold leaf on special issues of maps by the great mapmakers, rarely if ever on works by lesser cartographers. I remember some Blaeus I had, in full original hand color with gold leaf on the borders and in the cartouches. These were probably some of the most beautiful maps I've ever seen. Except, perhaps for the set of Cellarius star charts, published in the mid 1600's. Allegorical constellation figures, mythical beasts, maidens and chimeras fixed forever in the heavens. Portrayed on earth in some of the most beautiful plates ever engraved, they flamed with color and the power of their images was made immutable with gold leaf, the noble metal a talisman that warded off age, war and vandals. I shall never see printed images such as these again.

Purists recoil in horror at the idea of someone slobbering paint on a five hundred year old map. Quite honestly, I have mixed feelings about the practice. Unfortunately it is not a reversible act, and one of the cardinal rules in sound conservation practice is never to do anything that isn't reversible. Thus, when repairing a tear in paper, we use adhesives that are perfectly harmless and readily removable so that any future conservator can reverse what we've done without harming the artifact. Coloring, unfortunately is a one way street.

The process is simply painting with watercolors. No two prints so colored were ever exactly alike. Printed color is uniform, often made up of little dots visible under a magnifying glass. Absent are the brush strokes, the little runs and mistakes that are all part of hand coloring. Hand colorists were often paid by the piece. Audubon hired art students to color his lithographs. He paid them different amounts depending upon the job he wanted done. Some sets were to have better color than others and he paid accordingly. Larger publishers hired professional colorists who often sat in long rows, each applying one color to a print and then passing it along to the next person who applied the next color. Sort of a colorists' assembly line.

Coloring often follows cleaning. Maps and prints, like any physical item get dirty with the passing years. Sometimes they grow fungus or get waterstained. Grime and dampstaining do not, by themselves, threaten the piece, but fungus and mildew will ultimately ruin the paper. They should be dealt with and removed, much the same way woodworms should be killed when they infest a piece of antique furniture. Often the cleaning will include bleaching to remove stains and lighten the paper. Then the cleaned map gets its new colors. The result can often be difficult to tell from a well maintained, untreated map with original color. There is nothing wrong with repairing an artifact if it is needed, but some of these heroic efforts are analogous to stripping and bleaching a Governor Winthrop bureau, covering it with polyurethane varnish and replacing the

Uncommon Value

pulls. If you must do it, do it, but be honest about it and tell us you did it.

As the supply of old maps dries up and the more desirable of them disappear into collections, there is increasing economic pressure on dealers to repair, restore and color. If this is done openly nobody gets hurt. The collector can then make a decision about buying new color or not buying new color. It is often difficult to tell if color is recent because colorists and repair work have gotten very good in the past few years. Especially on the continent, where, even on inexpensive maps, I've seen completely new margins, restored corners and all new color. A quick glance would not have revealed this. Many of the Ortelius maps found on today's market in Europe have been cleaned and newly colored. Very well, at that. Most of the time we are able to tell old color from new, or at least be willing to put an opinion in writing. There are times when I cannot tell old from new with certainty, but by smelling (yes, smelling) the map, noting the degree of whiteness, the penetration of the colors, repair work, and the myriad of little clues and hints, at least present some educated structure to the problem. The final decision is always, of course, the client's.

More recently we are seeing some very well done new color that is virtually indistinguishable from the original. Much of this is originating in Europe. Many continental dealers have large stocks of newly colored maps that are quite well done. Although often not meant to deceive, modern color nonetheless should be indicated as such by the dealer and the map should not be passed off as having original color

Many dealers routinely send their uncolored maps to be colored. Even maps that were never meant to have color, such as the 19th century coastal charts issued by the United States Coast Survey have been colored in the name of marketability. Some of the results are dreadful and I shudder when I see them. Totally inappropriate color is often applied poorly and the practiced eye can spot it easily. Some dealers get reputations for having newly colored maps. Many of these are dealers who sell at antiques fairs rather than the big international book and map fairs, such as those sponsored by the ABAA. There is a less knowledgeable customer base at antiques fairs, since serious collectors usually don't buy there. It's where beginners, casual buyers and decorators get their maps. Unfortunately, many of these dealers don't admit that their maps are newly colored, when indeed, they should. There's a notorious pair of dealers who sell largely at antiques fairs who misrepresent their maps knowingly. They have stumbled onto the fact that a pseudo English accent helps sales. The best defense is always to get a written receipt that states the dealer's opinion of the color, and an explicit statement of the conservation or repair work done. You do have a good chance of getting your money back from a dealer if the item was misrepresented. The ABAA and our English counterpart, the ABA, has a Committee on Ethics and both organizations are pretty fussy about dealer honesty. A complaint to any of these organizations should bring swift results. If you have a serious problem with a dealer who isn't a member of these organizations, you can always contact the show's promoters. No promoter wants his show to get a bad rep, and any dealer who refuses to give written guarantees should, in my opinion, be avoided. Parenthetically, try getting a guarantee from an auction house.

By this point it should be clear that the price of any item is determined by a complex set of criteria. Without knowing these for a general area and also for a specific artifact, comparisons are difficult to make. You can shop around for the best price on an electronic gizmo or a camera, probably effect substantial savings and still get the identical product. It's much harder to determine equivalency of maps or books. This is especially true if you haven't dealt with a dealer before, or if you are looking up prices in a price guide. If you are a complete novice, a price guide will help you by telling you if a map is a hundred or a thousand dollar item. Or a five thousand dollar item. But a map listed in the latest edition at

Uncommon Value

$500. may be for sale for a thousand elsewhere and not be overpriced. Just recently I received a telephone call from a New Orleans dealer who wanted to know if I had any maps of his area. I had just gotten the 18th century Isaac Tirion map of New Orleans and the Mississippi delta region. Not a particularly scarce map, but a very nice one. My price to the dealer was $600. To my surprise he said he had to check his price guide. In it he found a price of $450. He didn't buy the copy I had. If a dealer has to rely on this kind of information to make decisions, he obviously hasn't got a good grasp of the market and the factors we just explored. The thirty-odd percent difference in prices is actually trivial and could be accounted for by any number of factors, including the fact that the price guide price was almost three years old.

Any specialist dealer should be able to tell you why he thinks a map or book is important and be able to compare its importance to other similar works. This places the item in its correct cultural context. A dealer who has to pull out some price guide to 'prove' what an item is 'worth' doesn't know his onions.

Chapter 4

Where did you get it?

███████████████████

Perhaps one of the most vexing and tiresome questions dealers get asked is "Where did you get this?" or the more general "Where do you buy your stock?

Sometimes it's no more than casual nicenoise, something that is said to fill a silence, sort of like "Have a nice day" or "How are you?" Often, it's a question of curiosity from someone who has never seen an assemblage of antiquarian items. Old, to some of these people is 1945. A roomfull of stuff from 1745 or earlier is virtually unbelievable. Really, where do we get this stuff?

Then, of course, is the crafty individual who asks the question quite casually, in the hopes that we'll spill the beans and let him in on the secret source of our cheap buys. This will let him go to the same place and circumvent the middleman.

The map dealer, George Ritzlin, tired of this question, wrote a marvelous little article dealing with the source of dealers' inventory. He invented the legend of the "Bookdealers' Warehouse" located somewhere in Kansas. This place was wonderful, a booksellers' Schlarraffenland. Every rare book and map dealer was a member of the

Uncommon Value

warehouse association. Whenever a dealer was offered an item, he would place it in the warehouse. Then, he would have credit with the warehouse and would be able to take inventory from it that he needed for his own business. Thus, the mythical warehouse was sort of a cooperative repository. George had his little article published in a trade magazine and we all thought it great fun. Over the years, however, George has received many inquiries asking the address of the warehouse! So great is the belief in some mystical source for our inventory that this sort of question will never die, nor can it be ever answered - we won't be believed.

By 'buying' I mean me buying. Buying for inventory, for resale. We dealers buy from many sources, including auctions, other dealers and private parties. There is a link between buying and selling. On an obvious level, one has to get things in order to sell them. So much for the question we are often asked: "Do you buy books?" The temptation is enormous whenever I am asked this, or a variant of this question.

The most direct way to acquire inventory, of course, is to buy it from a private owner who wants to sell. Usually an individual will contact a dealer and ask if he wants to buy something. Having an open shop or a 'real' office is invaluable because it creates a legitimacy in the public's mind. You're a 'real' dealer if you have public space. Also, one's space makes a statement. It makes an economic statement and a class statement. Sellers, as well as buyers, must feel comfortable with whom they do business. This is especially so in this business where trust is important. It's been my experience that the basis of this trust is established almost immediately at first contact between client and dealer. The client will enter one's premises and casually look around. One glance will tell someone a lot about the establishment. What's on the floors is as important as what's on the walls. Everything makes a statement. Of course one has to back up an initial quality statement with quality action.

F.J. Manasek

An elderly lady come in with a globe she wanted to sell. She had seen one of our ads in an antiques magazine and brought in a very nice little dissected globe. A dissected globe is a globe puzzle. Essentially a wooden globe cut into pies or slices along lines of latitude and each 'pie' then cut into wedge shaped pieces. All the pieces are covered with printed paper and can be assembled into coherent pies, and the pies in turn can be reassembled into the globe. These are 19th century items and fall somewhere between toys and teaching aids. This was very pretty little example about five inches in diameter and in like-new condition. It was German, made for the English export market in about 1850. I offered her well over a thousand dollars for it. She began to stammer and I thought that I had offended her with the offer - perhaps someone had told her she should get more. Indeed, just the opposite was true. She had sold a similar piece not too long ago to an antiques dealer for a hundred dollars. The story came out. She needed money; she could no longer work and she was selling off several generations of things that remained in her family house. Unfortunately she had already sold off many valuable items, including a pair of library globes, for a pittance. I am not sure if I did her a favor by paying her a fair price for her dissected globe - she was crying as she left my office, weeping with the realization that she had been cheated. Perhaps she should not have learned this. At least not from me.

Wearing worn, but once-fine clothing, another elderly lady walked into my office. She had called earlier to make certain I would be there. "I've had this a long time," she said. "and now is the time for me to sell it. I have some expenses coming up and I can use the money."

She unwrapped a sheet of vellum. An ordinary English legal document from the 17th century. "I've been saving this for when I might need the money." Tidy and proud, her worn clothing still spoke of better days. They too, were reserved for important occasions such as this one. "See," they seemed to say "I cost a lot of money. I am quality. I haven't always been worn and threadbare."

Alas, she had been mistaken. Her hopes were misplaced and her ace in the hole, her Sunday-punch, her little secret for a rainy day was virtually worthless. I felt dreadful when I finally had to tell her I wasn't interested in buying it.

"It's very old." she pointed out to me, as though I hadn't seen. "Why, it was written just a few years after the Declaration of Independence. It's almost as old as our country. It must be very valuable. I think it must be worth several thousand."

I tried to be as gentle as I could yet explain to her at the same time that it wasn't worth very much at all. I hesitated to put a figure to it, for fear of making her feel worse than necessary.

"How much do you think it's worth?" she asked, "Can I get, say a thousand dollars for it?" The figure was no longer plural. This was obviously much less than she had in mind when she decided to sell it, but was clearly willing to take what she thought a ridiculously low price. "Sorry, I don't think so. Not nearly."

"Well then," and her voice became stronger, her resolution manifest, doubtless as in earlier days. She clearly meant no nonsense; I needn't trifle with her. "Just how much?"

How to tell her? Those few shreds of diplomacy that had groped their way into my being were inadequate. There was no way to tell her without hurting. "These aren't very valuable, really," I said. "I can buy them in England for very little money. They're quite common. And this one isn't very old. They mostly have a decorative value."

"Would you give me five hundred dollars?"

"I'm sorry, they can be bought for less than $50.00 in England." I finally had to say it.

"What would you give me for it?" I think she believed

me, and realized that I wasn't trying to cheat her. At least I hope so.

"I would rather not. I'm sorry, but I really can't use it, even at a very low price." Indeed, such documents were available in England for a few pounds but I would not want to buy hers - she might always have harbored a suspicion that it was indeed her fortune and that she had been done out of it.

In answer to her questions, I assured her I was quite certain I knew what I was talking about and that I was not mistaken. Also, she might try selling it to an antiques dealer or putting it into an auction - in either case she might get lucky.

Through her dignity her disappointment penetrated as profoundly as any I'd ever seen. I suspect she'd held on to this document for a rainy day, knowing that it would save her. Now her day was rainy and her dream had been dampened. She left looking a good deal older, more tired. Her clothing, old friends to the end, having conspired with her to dignify her entry shared with her the disappointment and tried hard to ease her exit. Which they did. I felt worse than she.

The type of vellum document she offered for sale is really quite common, but not well known. Legal events, especially land transactions were recorded since written time immemorial. Incised clay tablets. Papyrus to pergamin. Papyrus sheets, made of individual papyrus plant leaves woven into flat sheets, sized and trimmed, were used widely for written documents and 'books' in the middle east Papyrus sheets were exported to other regions, a very active trade. Their production and export were controlled by the government of Egypt and by regulating the monopoly the government realized a substantial income. In an attempt to raise prices and squeeze more money out of the product, export was limited by decree. In response, in the west, the import of papyrus was curtailed and an animal product was substituted. This was parchment, or vellum. It was also

Uncommon Value

known as 'pergamin' named after the city known for its production. Indeed, it is still called *pergamino* in Spain. Parchment is a product manufactured from animal skins. Cow, sheep, ox, calf. They were all used to produce pergamin, or vellum, or parchment of different qualities. The skins were stretched on frames, rubbed with lime to absorb and remove the oils and fats and then scraped with large, curved scraping tools. This removed the hair from the outside and the connective tissue, or subdermis, from the inside. After suitable drying and curing, the skins, now parchment, were cut to size and sold to the scribes. Each sheet of parchment made from mature animals has one side darker than the other. The darker side is the original 'inside' of the animal; the lighter side the 'outside' of the skin. In general, the inside or darker surface is the oilier and often shows more signs of age and wear since the oilier surface makes it more difficult for the ink to adhere to the parchment. Often it flakes off, making the text difficult to read. Large animals were needed to produce large sheets of vellum. Thus, the very large antiphonals, such as those characteristic of the late 17th and early 18th centuries, were made of ox vellum, a rather coarse product. The very finest books' pages were made of a very delicate vellum, almost as thin as onion skin paper. This vellum was derived from the skins of fetal lamb or fetal calf. Animals were bred and slaughtered for the skins of their unborn. Embryonic and fetal connective tissue is not as robust as its mature counterpart. There are quantitative changes that take place early in post-natal life, but there are also qualitative changes. The type of collagen, from the standpoint of its amino acid composition and the molecule as a specific gene product is different. Moreover, collagens and other substituents of the connective tissue such as the glycosaminoglycans and the glycoproteins undergo molecular 'aging' and develop cross-links as the animal ages. All this changes the physical characteristics of the vellum. I always marvel at the softness of the pages made of fetal vellum; the purity of their color and fineness of grain. Quality fetal vellum doesn't show the pronounced inside/outside color differences that vellums from older animals show. Perhaps we should remember that most of the fetal vellum leaves, a product of a giant medieval industry, were incorporated into books to be read by ladies, who left no written accounts of their maternal affiliations with their ovine sisters who were exploited for their unborn.

Northern New England has been in sort of a recession since the end of the Civil War when the railroads finally opened up the west. It was no longer economical to farm the rocky hillsides, fight the short growing seasons and the spring muds that followed the winter snows. Ohio and lands beyond had fertile soil deep to infinity and didn't sprout a crop of rocks each winter. Other, perhaps more global, economic forces conspired to kill the mills, and more recently, in my own day, finish off the last of the shoemaking industry.

The losses, first of farming and later of industry, have harmed the area in one sense by reducing the number of salaried jobs. In the greater sense it has saved New England from being homogenized and blighted the way much of the rest of the country has been. Vermont still has a total state population of under a million (although people now outnumber cows); New Hampshire a bit more but about the same. We are more forested now than at any time since colonial days. Only recently is there a large enough population base for the likes of Wal-Mart to try to come in. They are trying and we are resisting. The fringes of our towns and little cities haven't all been ringed by split level suburbs leaving a main street of shuttered shops. Eight-lane superhighways don't dissect us and integrity still lurks among the populace, like some vestigial memory, rising to the occasion when required and making life rather pleasant all around. The term "moral fiber," archaic in the rest of the country, still has meaning here.

There is a downside to this, and that is the lack of steady work for blue-collar workers. There is some seasonal building, but not that much since the population is not

Uncommon Value

growing very rapidly. When the national economy sneezes, we are in trouble. But the qualities that make life good are still here and those who treasure these remain, learn to adapt, and thrive on the respect from their neighbors. Nonetheless, they still need to eat, and the trouble is, one can't eat respect and esteem.

The very nice, spare man, in his early thirties, had such trouble. He looked hungry, not in young Cassius' sense, but in the sense that he hadn't eaten. He came into my Hanover office early one Saturday afternoon, just before I was about to pack it in for the week. With him were his two daughters, about seven and eight. There was already a nip in the air but all three were dressed only lightly. The children's pale, anemic look, their print dresses and their father's work clothes all reminded me of those dust-bowl, depression years photographs and I felt a strength come into the office along with this family. The girls smiled shyly at me and giggled when I thumbed my nose at them. Spotting the group of library globes standing in the middle of the floor, one of them started spinning the 1812 Cary globe. The "Please Do Not touch" sign, as we all know, didn't mean little girls. Her father caught my eye and eased her away from the globe. "Pretty expensive item? I bet I can't even guess" he volunteered. "That one's worth a new pick-up." He held onto his daughter a bit more tightly.

"Can I show you this map, maybe see how much it's worth?"

He unrolled a worn, early 20th Century plan of Hanover and Dartmouth College. The plan had been done as a student exercise at the Thayer School of Engineering. Inwardly I groaned. Again, my resolve to be a businessman would be tested, again I would lose. I knew it. He was hungry, his kids were hungry. I was not. I offered him a hundred bucks for the thing. He took it, but not before expressing some of his Yankee trader genes. "Can you make it any more?" "Sorry, wish I could." I gave him cash.

F.J. Manasek

Two years later I finally sold the ugly thing for fifty dollars, but considering the overall profit I made, I think I got a good deal.

I used to visit a second-hand book dealer who's pretty well known. He has a nice shop in a nice old house and plays the right kind of music softly. He gets 'scouted' a lot by other dealers who find, consistently, vastly underpriced books on his shelves. They hold him in mild contempt but nonetheless patronize his shop because of the bargains to be found. "I hope old Jim Fistula doesn't wake up" was the oft repeated comment.

Years ago I used to visit him and wile away time chatting, or rather listening to him, he had an oral compulsion to expound on every topic. I too, got some great bargains from him. Although Jim had been in the book business for some years, he never figured it out. For example he priced a fine copy of the first edition of Horblit's *Hundred Books Famous In Science* at twenty dollars. It was a hundred dollar book at the time. Great deal if you were a buyer, but as I said to a client, "Would you want your widow to sell him your library?" Someone's bargain is always someone else's loss.

Jim used popular price guides to price his books. If a book wasn't listed in his *Pocket Guide To Book Prices* or *Fortune in Your Attic Bookcase* or some other similar drivel he was at a loss. The late Sean Moyne, a much respected bookseller in Putney, Vermont was vociferous on this topic and when I first moved to the area warned me. I discounted the warning, but recalled it one day after I had picked out some books from Jim's inventory, I remembered an errand I had promised to do. "Run me up an invoice on these, will you," I said as I left, the pile of books on his counter, "I'll be back in an hour." When I got back to pick up the books, some prices had been changed. Upward, of course. I paid the invoice and never returned to the shop.

We all make mistakes and either pay too much or too little for things that come our way. Most of us try to minimize the spread and pay fair market prices. My own failing is that I try to compensate too much and probably, over time, pay more for my inventory than I should. Sometimes I've gone in the other direction. I was asked to look at a small collection of loose prints, some old masters and some old minors. A bit out of my field, but I thought I'd try to buy them in. I was a bit nervous about them so I underestimated them. The owner's children convinced her not to sell them to me, probably thinking me a crook of some sort. I'm just as glad she didn't let me buy them, I would have had trouble selling them since they weren't my specialty. I only hope she didn't think I was trying to flim-flam her.

Sunshine to a dealer's dull day are those occasions when someone will bring in one or more very good books or maps, announce them for sale, agree to a fair price and leave, lighter in goods but larger in pocketbook.

Certain to dim an otherwise bright morning are the people who come in with mounds of detritus that they've been told are worth jillions. Often, these people have, being very clever folk, contacted the big-city auction houses such as Christoby's. "Ah, yes," says some bright, perfumed lad, who knows only that a book has covers, "this is worth a great deal. We are so glad you've shown it to us, but it is not our specialty. I suggest you sell it to a dealer. It's worth several thousand dollars, at least." Armed with this knowledge, the expectant owner lugs the stuff in to us dealers and waits for the rain of coinage. Alas, not to be. "I'm sorry, sir, despite what Christoby's have told you, the second volume of a five volume set of Thackery isn't much sought after. Yes, I know it's very old, why 1936 was well before the war."

This complaint is particularly common in England. Time and again I've heard dealers voice essentially the same refrain. It seems to follow a formula and I wouldn't be surprised if there truly is some grand scheme to discredit dealers. I'm quite convinced it's in the best interests of the auction houses to undermine the credibility of dealers. We compete for the same market.

The same is happening in this country, but possibly to a lesser extent. Even small rural auctions are puffing themselves up and advertising that they are getting fantastic prices for consignments. Sometimes they do indeed, but mostly they do not. The whole issue with buying and selling at auction is very complex, but just as dealers have difficulty getting good inventory, auctions have similar problems. They have become huge juggernauts, consuming huge amounts of non-replenishable goods, and they have to keep getting them. I think they have tried to do this at the expense of dealers. Some of our British cousins in the antiques trade have begun to strike back. I know a number of dealers who, when they get someone coming in with a vanload of rubbish they say: "You have some really nice items here, but I'm afraid out of our league. There's quite a specialty market in old edentulous celluloid combs and I suggest you take them to Christoby's. I'm sure you will be surprised." Tit for tat.

Chapter 5

Dealers

Dealers come in many flavors. There are the great dealers of the past, such as the legendary Rosenbach. And there are the great legends of today such as the Chicago dealer Harry Stern who has the reputation of being one of the most honorable dealers active today. There is the Pennsylvania dealer, Graham Arader, probably one of the most well-know American dealers, having been featured in stories in the Wall Street Journal. There are numerous other 'characters' in the trade, many of whom operate large successful businesses with clients throughout the world. Some, of course, are quite the opposite, and haven't the foggiest idea how to run a business.

I used to get a fellow in my Hanover shop who identified himself as a preacher and also a book dealer. Invariably, after making his clerical ties known, he would stand back a bit and puff out his chest, just a bit, and wait for me to be impressed beyond all belief.

"What sort of books do you deal with?"

"Well, I travel a lot preaching, and I see who has things that my clients might want." At which point he would take out a pad and begin listing our titles, asking "How much would you want for that one? Dealer price, of course?"

51

F.J. Manasek

Seems this fellow wandered about the country selling his god and second hand books. He knew very little about books and I doubt that he ever sold a single one. He probably knew even less about God and religion, but no doubt that sold quite well. I don't think I ever knew his name, but he came in quite often and seemed not to remember that he had been in before. Same story, same pitch, same hurt look when I told him I didn't let people make lists of my inventory. Fiona never understood my objections to that practice. She always thought that someday one of these guys would sell one of our books.

At the very least, this sort of practice represents an effort to run a business using someone else's capital and knowledge. They assume that I know what I'm doing because I have four-figure books on the shelf and that all they need to do is let their imaginary clients know about them and, hey Presto, they've made a sale and a fat profit without investing any of their own money. At the worst, it is an effort to make a list of someone's inventory, especially the better books, get them priced and then come in at night and steal them to order.

This sort of negative experience aside, it was usually very pleasant to entertain visiting dealers. Most dealers know their stuff and make decisions very quickly. One doesn't have to 'sell' them.

Beginning with the mid 1980's I noticed an increase in the number of foreign dealers who visited the United States in order to buy inventory. I didn't get my share of them since Hanover is a bit off the beaten path, but when they did come through they always bought well.

I was in Spain visiting friends on the Bay of Biscay when Paul Nicholas came to Hanover on a buying trip. Paul had had a shop in London but decided to move to the States where the action was. He and his wife Mona planned to settle in Hawaii and open a gallery there. Paul was making the rounds looking for inventory. Fiona let him browse and he bought some very nice items, including several spectacular Buddhist pieces. But Paul was looking for 19th century American atlases and we had none. Fiona suggested he contact Ron Blumenthal, a dealer located a few hours' drive from Hanover. Paul called Ron and asked him if he had any atlases. Indeed, he had, said Ron, and Paul was welcome to come out and look. This was not on Paul's itinerary and represented a three hundred mile detour, but he needed the atlases. Paul paid Fiona for the items he bought from me, loaded them into his rented car and drove off to see Blumenthal. Months later, at the San Francisco fair I had lunch with Paul and asked him if he had gotten any atlases from Ron. Paul got a strange expression. Apparently he found Ron's house (he worked out of his home) and had a pleasant chat. Ron didn't have any maps that Paul wanted and Paul asked to see the atlases. Ron brought them out and Paul examined them.

"I'd like to buy them." said Paul. "How much?"

"Oh, these aren't for sale. I'm saving these for my retirement." was Ron's response.

Billy Sterling breezed in one day. I hadn't known Billy, he had a shop in New York State and we had never done business together. Billy identified himself as a dealer and asked if he could look around. "Of course," I responded, "if there's anything you'd like to see, I'd be pleased to show you." A few minutes later, Billy stomped into my office. "How can you make a living with such a small inventory?" Billy, it turned out, was a dealer who sold inexpensive used books and ephemera. He dealt in trade cards, valentines, and lots of books in the twenty dollar range. The percentage profit in these items is large, but the dollar amount is small so a dealer like Billy needs to have a large inventory and turn it over rapidly. He was shocked at my small premises and my small book inventory, probably at that time around five hundred volumes. Our two businesses were so different that the only thing they had in common was that we both dealt in old paper items. There was nothing in my shop that Billy could have bought for his inventory. The reverse was not necessarily true. It is possible, that I might have found some suitable items in Billy's shop had I scouted it. I can often find real gems hidden away in such shops. Indeed, many of the items in my inventory are bought in just this way, from general used book dealers.

There's a food chain in this business, and the lower-end dealers, like plankton, extract nutrients from the vast ocean around us. Different dealers occupy niches along the food chain. Books and maps are traded along this food chain, ultimately reaching the level of their buoyant density. Middle and upper range dealers tend not to buy lower range goods, so although dealers who specialize in the lower price ranges often don't find anything higher up in the food chain, they often get in better items for which they do not have retail customers. These items get sold upward in the trade. It's always worth scouting dealers' shops when traveling.

Members of the trade have a curious symbiotic relationship. We depend upon each other heavily. We are constantly buying and selling inventory from and to each other. Yet we compete for customers. By and large, I don't think that the collecting base is expanding. It is, to use a business school term, a "mature market." Therefore we each grow at someone else's expense. It's not as though I invent a better product that creates a new market and therefore prosper. If my business prospers it's because I'm selling to customers who aren't buying from someone else. Yet we dealers remain remarkably civil to each other and even refer customers. Perhaps the best aspect of the trade is the trust that exists among dealers. I'm constantly amazed when someone sends me a packet of maps on approval and discover the postman has just delivered fifty thousand dollars worth of maps on the basis of a telephone call. But then, I've got at least that amount out on approval to other dealers. It's because of this overall congeniality that we find the exceptions so interesting.

Among these exceptions, I've observed, are some dealers in children's books. For some reason this is a

Uncommon Value

remarkably competitive lot and in some`parts of the trade there surfaces an enormous amount of back-stabbing, rumor-mongering and ill-will. It's a charming thought that the dear sweet lady who has just replaced your childhood copies of *Dumbo* and *The Little Ducklings and their Fuzzy Friends* has just screwed the foo out of her colleague, who in turn is plotting her own revenge!

It's very rare for a dealer to stiff another dealer, but it happens. The major bookseller associations have ethics committees to resolve such disputes and miscreants can be expelled from the association. Most effective, though, is the Jungle Telegraph. We all depend so heavily upon the honesty of our peers that any fall from grace gets transmitted rather quickly. Most remarkable are the few bad apples who have dreadful credit ratings, some of whom have been expelled from the organization, and whom everyone knows to be beyond trust, yet who continue to survive, even grow.

Hendry Corrado was one of these. Hendry, a delightful Continental scoundrel, is world famous for his rubber checks. Everyone in the trade knows this, and I'm always amazed when I hear new stories of how he is again being chased by some dealer. The amounts are often substantial. He once owed a dealer DM80,000. and wrote at least three bad checks to him. Ultimately, he paid. Hendry deals in a stratospheric level of very rare, very expensive maps. I occasionally bought the odd map from him, but haven't in some time because I'm worried about title. I don't know who Hendry has stiffed to get the maps he's selling and some day one of his stiffees is going to go to Interpol. Some have expressed doubt Hendry has clear title to some of his maps.

Louis is a major South American collector. He has one of the biggest collections of South American maps in private hands. He stiffs dealers and lets them twist in the wind for months before paying them. I've got him on a cash only basis, no check, no map. I heard a story, perhaps not true but delightful anyway. A couple of dealers, tired of trying to collect from Louis, had Hendry act as intermediary in a big transaction with Louis. They sold the maps to Hendry for cash (possibly why the story doesn't ring entirely true) who sold them to Louis who stiffed Hendry.

There was a wonderful drama a few years ago that unfolded on the pages of national newspapers, as well as trade journals. There had been a theft of some large Audubon folio bird prints from a New Orleans museum. These are very expensive items, some individual prints fetching well into five figures. The police allegedly traced some of the hot prints to a dealer and when they tried to recover them, were told that they had been 'beyond repair' and that the conservator had cut them up to use the paper for other things. There was a wave of raucous laughter that girdled the earth when this appeared in the papers. The prints, surprisingly, were "found" soon after.

I recently encountered a dreadful little part-time dealer in northern Florida. Rastam Firdani was one of those pseudo-dealers who liked to get as much material as possible 'on approval' and then run around showing it to potential buyers. Meanwhile, he would behave as objectionably as possible, whining about the price, whining about the condition of the items he had, whining about payment terms, always offering less than the agreed price, and all the while distancing himself from the starting proposition that he had to pay. Rastam had snookered me. He had gotten several of my nicest Arabic manuscripts with the promise to pay me the next week. Every few days he would call to tell me that he needed more time, that there was another problem with one of the manuscripts, that his 'brother' (Rastam never admitted to being a dealer; he claimed he was showing these things to his family) was out of town, that his father was ill and a myriad of other excuses. They were all designed to distance himself from the very concept that he owed money to me. It became clear that he was was going to try to stiff me. To try to recover the money by hiring a lawyer to represent me two thousand miles away would be folly beyond that exhibited by me in sending Rastam the manuscripts in the first place. Rastam thought he had pulled a perfect sting on me. However, I decided to sting him back. I don't think con artists ever expect their victims to con them back. This victim did. I called Rastam and let him know that I had more manuscripts. They were very special, one of them was a Persian Sha-na-ma that I kept in the vault; there were several vellum leaves of Kufic Koranic text from very early in the history of Islam and numerous other items of similar value. I sent Rastam a few Polaroids of some minor things, letting him know that the big items would be photographed in due course. I would send him these treasures to "look at" after he paid me for the first lot. Rastam fumed, whined, wheedled and tried to make excuses. He sometimes telephoned me several times in an afternoon and tried to tell me that everything was my fault.

"Can't we just do everything as a single deal? Can't you send me these to look at and in the meantime I'll send you a check for the other manuscripts? Why are you being so difficult. I do not do business this way. Everyone trusts me. You are the only one who does not. Whine Whine."

Meanwhile, the Jungle Telegraph was at work. Seems that Rastam was doing this to other dealers. He had a lot of stuff from several other manuscript dealers and was playing the same game. I remained adamant. Pay what you owe and I'll send you the Sha-na-ma on approval. Rastam sent me a check that cleared! But it was a few hundred dollars short. "I'll send the rest to you when I get the Sha-na-ma." promised Rastam.

"Sorry, but I'll send you the other stuff when I get full payment."

Full payment arrived. I was elated. I had pulled off the reverse sting! Rastam, on the other hand, was convinced he had set me up for the big kill. By paying me the ten thousand he owed on the first transaction, he thought he would get my Kufic leaves and Sha-na-ma on approval, items worth possibly a hundred thousand dollars. Then he could pull the big one. Needless to say, I never sent another thing to

Rastam. I think after about his fifth telephone call to me, he realized what had happened and he never called again. He knew I would never do business with him even if he paid me up front in Krugerrands. The Islamic manuscripts were beautiful sacred texts and should never have gotten into the hands of that little snake. Hopefully, no more will. *Inshallah.*

By and large our clan's a good one. We earn our living buying and selling as well as providing services, so we have to buy for less than we sell. Just how much less is a sticky issue. When does making a large profit become fraud, theft or some other heinous act? Courts have ruled in many cases that a dealer cannot deceive someone who is trying to sell an item. I think this is still a very difficult gray area, but also believe that there is some sort of a fair markup. Dealers buying from each other within the trade represent a very different type of transaction. If someone sets himself up as a dealer; calls himself a dealer, has business cards and stationery, then I believe him. To me, this is prima facie evidence that he knows what he is doing and if he vastly undervalues something it is not my responsibility to tell him. It's a very different situation when the proverbial little old lady comes into my shop and wants to sell an item that she doesn't know is valuable. It is my responsibility then, to let her know what she has and make an offer commensurate. There are some who disagree.

About a year ago, in a town to the west of me, an elderly lady took a letter to a local auctioneer. The letter had been in her family for generations, having been written by George Washington to one of her ancestors. The letter had never been published, it had never been examined by scholars or historians. It was completely 'fresh'. The owner, last in her line, needed money to make some much needed repairs to her house, pay some bills and provide a bit of creature comfort in her declining years. The auctioneer managed to buy in the letter for about $7000. He immediately sold it to a specialist manuscript dealer for about $40,000. In an effort to get more information about the letter, the manuscript dealer traced it back to the original seller who soon discovered the real value of what she had sold. Needless to say the lawyers are going to eat well on this one. Fortunately for the victim in this case there is an infrastructure to protect her. The ABAA has an ethics committee that is very powerful. No dealer wants to be expelled from the ABAA; it's the mark of Cain. Regional book dealers' associations are there to help her and, of course, there's the state Attorney General. Most states have laws against this kind of behavior. At least when it involves dealers. There's another set of rules for auction houses.

At the time I'm writing this, there is yet no resolution to the question of the George Washington letter. But I'm sure there will be. This auctioneer is an unsavory sort, someone with whom I've never had a really satisfactory transaction. I stopped trying to deal with him years ago. Perhaps others will also.

Fortunately, for every dealer like this in the field there are a hundred honorable and reputable ones who give fair prices and who treat people fairly. There are legends in the field, dealers who have sent checks for thousands of dollars to individuals whose property has turned out to be worth much more than supposed. I remember in particular the New York City dealer who, in the course of buying some prints from a lady in Maine, got a large group of clipper ship cards. This wasn't his field, he didn't know much about them, but when he found out, he sent her a check for $20,000. As I recall, someone told me he wound up making about 10% on the deal. With colleagues such as these, I don't think we should wear hair shirts because of the rascals among us, we should simply expel them from the clan.

Chapter 6

Breaking and faking

Atlases don't live forever. Sometimes they succumb to the natural ravages of time. Mice, rain, war and fire consume their share. One of my clients lost several great atlases in the recent California fires. Another enemy of the atlas is the dreaded "breaker." Breakers are dealers who take apart books for their separate contents. The word breaker sometimes refers to the book itself, as in "This book is in such poor condition that it's an easy breaker."

I recently bought an early 1600's edition of Magini's atlas. This is not a particularly beautiful atlas, but has several important maps including a couple of very nice world maps. The front (fortunately) third had been water damaged to the point where the paper was soft and pulpy. Several pages had come apart and large pieces of the soft paper were missing. The title page was missing and the top board warped and damaged beyond repair. What to do with such a book? I sold it to a dealer who was going to separate ("break") it for the maps that were still in good condition.

Is this wrong? One can argue it both ways. On one hand, breaking this book will separate it forever. Those of us who were brought up to treasure the book will wince a bit. I remember scribbling in a book as a child. Just once. I also remember the day we would get our new books at the beginning of each new school term. That night my mother would help me cover each book with a jacket of brown paper. Corners were given a second cover of brown paper. At the end of the school year, when we returned our books, I was proud that mine were always in the best condition. As a matter of fact, I noticed that those of us who were the best students and, presumably, used our books the most, always returned them in good condition. I noticed also, that the kids who were not good students, and who used books little or not at all, were the ones who returned them in dreadful condition. Although I have a long standing respect for the physical integrity of books, I can't get too upset about the practice of "breaking" damaged books. In the case of my Magini, the one I sold into the boneyard, there was no way that it could have been restored at any sensible price. One can hope for the odd chance of finding another similar edition with the back part damaged and then "marrying" the good parts of each. Indeed, this is sometimes possible and I have often been called upon to provide the odd map that someone needed to "complete" an atlas. Some books appear to lose specific pages. Peter Apian's *Cosmographia* is one of these. It was published with a wooodblock world map. The map fetches a good price and many times is removed from the book to be sold as a separate item. The book, otherwise intact, is sold into the book market. Someone buys it and wants to replace the missing map and we map dealers get the call. Almost invariably the separate map will cost more than the completed book is worth. I don't really understand these economics, but they are real. In the case of the Magini, had I been able to find another copy with the salvageable parts that I needed, I probably could have effected a marriage, but certainly not at a profit since the resulting grafted volume would not be worth very much.

On the other hand, years ago, dealers would break perfectly sound atlases. I shudder to think of the Blaeu, the Hondius, and the Mercator atlases that went to the knackers. The great Ronald Vere Tooley, who did so much for the field of map collecting, could run his thumbnail down a page and deftly remove a map in a single, smooth motion. Graham Arader, that well known American dealer who appears in news articles from time to time, used to sell shares in sumptuous volumes. These were very expensive folio works, each costing many thousands or many tens of thousands of dollars. Graham would then hold breaking parties, where each shareholder would get his or her plates from the folios. Quite a festive occasion, no doubt.

Breaking occurs only when there is economic incentive. Sundown dealers, the mom-and-pop map and printsellers do this with a vengeance with lower-end items. One can still buy a late nineteenth century atlas for around a hundred dollars. Take it apart and sell the maps to collectors for fifty bucks a pop and you've made a thousand dollars. True, it takes forever to get rid of some of the dogs, but if you're doing this on weekends and holidays it's more of a hobby than livelihood and time doesn't matter quite as much. As I said elsewhere, all it takes is a hundred bucks and a razor blade.

Better volumes are no longer breakable at a profit. One can no longer buy a nice Blaeu atlas and take it apart and sell off the components for enough money to make the exercise worthwhile. The price of the atlas has gone so high that many mom and pop dealers cannot afford the sixty thousand or more to buy one and they cannot afford to borrow the money to buy one — it takes too long to sell the parts and the profit isn't there to make it worthwhile. This is sparing the atlases from further breaking. One occasionally still does find the damaged item that can be broken, but more often than not it is priced on the basis of its "breaker" value, and not priced as a damaged atlas.

Atlases aren't the only books to feel the edge of the blade. Botanicals have, in the recent past, been taken apart with remarkable fervor, their leaves falling like foreskins in Ramadan. I think the craze for botanicals really took off over decade ago when magazines such as *Architectural Digest*

Uncommon Value

and that Peoria of American interior design, *House Beautiful,* began to show interiors with botanical prints on the walls. Decorators took the bit and galloped with it, and every botanical from Dr. Thornton's *Temple of Flora* to Anne Pratt's pretty little chromos felt the swish of the liberating steel. Shells, insects and mammals were also dragged from the library and put against the wall. Birds, especially the Goulds, Audubons and *Parrots in Captivity* went next.

There's nothing new about taking books apart for their illustrations. Perhaps the greatest impetus to disbind was given by James Granger, an English clergyman of the eighteenth century. Granger encouraged the addition of portraits and other illustrations to existing books. Naturally, these illustrations all came from other books. The Grangerites went on a rampage. Thousands of books were disbound to provide fodder for the Grangerized products. The price of portraits increased as the mania spread. Perhaps not until Americans began buying prints in huge piles in this century, were prices affected as dramatically. Fortunately, Grangerizing, or 'extra-illustrating' has lost fashion and although grangerized works do attract some attention at sales, few more are being made. The mania has run its course.

Illustrated books were priced modestly before the decorating craze took over. I recall that as late as the 1970's, it was possible to buy them for modest amounts and even several of the minor auction houses had regular sales of illustrated books. At about that time, there appeared on the auction scene in New York, an elderly man, a retired plumber, if I'm correct, who began buying illustrated books like crazy. He attended all the Swann sales, sat in the front row, stuck up his hand at the start of bidding and kept it up. He bought tons of books, some perfect copies, most damaged, all illustrated and all old and lovely. After each sale, he'd put them in the back of his pickup truck and go home to New Jersey. His children, fearing that the old guy had lost his marbles and was squandering their birthright, had him declared incompetent and put a stop to his buying adventures. Too bad! Everything he bought appreciated faster than the stock market and they could have been quite well off had they let the ex-plumber spend a bit more.

Maps are high on the decorators' wish lists. We've been noticing them on the walls of 'perfect rooms' in the right magazines and there is strong decorator interest. I get calls from decorators in the big cities who, crafty persons, know that because I'm in Vermont I get things very cheap and don't know prices. They are looking for "big, colorful maps of America, very old and pretty, and not too expensive." I generally send them an old catalogue of mine. I often get a telephone call back, asking about some long-sold item, usually one that is very big, very old, colorful, scarce and expensive. Before I can even tell them its gone, they ask "How much off for me. I'm a decorator." I've learned. My answer is "Ten percent, I'll send it to you upon receipt of your check." Invariably there are howls of dismay. "I always get at least forty percent, mostly sixty percent. I need several of these, send them to me so I can pick them out. I'll need to show them to my clients." Translation: "I deal in reproductions, I'll keep them for six months or so, maybe send some back, probably not sell any at all, but if I do, you can whistle for your money." I am perfectly happy to let other dealers deal with decorators. Years ago I shared space in Chicago's Merchandise Mart, that ultimate experience in decorating accessories. Indeed, there is big money in selling genuine items into the decorating trade, but it needs a different personality than mine. I pulled out.

The botanical craze seems to have run its course, or at least abated a bit. One of the things that caused it to slow down is the price escalation of the old botanical prints. When the originals got pricey enough, some very fine reproductions began to appear on the market. Although printed by offset lithography, the better repros are hand colored and look pretty enough. An experienced eye can tell they weren't real but most decorators' clients cannot. Repros are priced sufficiently low to displace the real thing, especially when size and color were the determinants. So much of decorating involves getting something "just the right color." What it is is of secondary importance. Repros are certainly good enough in many cases.

This is happening with maps as well. Prices of some of the great Americas maps, such as the Blaeu and Speed are up above six thousand dollars. At these prices, one can afford to make very good repros and still compete in the decorative market. I get a few calls each month asking about reproductions. I don't deal in them and don't know where to get them. Few callers believe this and simply cannot understand that I, as a map dealer, don't sell copies.

The whole question of reproductions is a tricky one. Fortunately few of the reproductions currently on the market were made as forgeries; they were mostly produced as colorful copies of the originals. There is no problem if the repro is done by a technique different from the one that was used to make the original. I can spot a lithographed reproduction of an old copperplate engraved map from across the room. The average owner of such a reproduction is often unconvinced that it isn't original, especially if it's in a fancy old frame. I think some antique dealers put them into old frames with appropriately stained mats and dirty glass. I've seen several where the mats were of a wrong size. Printed color is generally a dead giveaway. Until the development of lithography, maps were all colored by hand. Indeed, all the great old illustrations, botanical, zoological, scenery, city views as well as maps were also colored by hand.

Indeed, there are a number of different reproductions that appear in the market with some regularity. An insurance company, in the 1950's, I believe, issued a large format calendar with illustrations of Audubon birds. Nicely done, many of these seem to have been saved and framed for use as decoration. Several times a year some of these would be brought to me for possible purchase. I would try to explain that they were not original Audubons but I was often not believed. As one person told me, "My grandmother had these on her wall and she only had good things." They've been around long enough to have taken on a life and credibility of their own. I occasionally see them in antique shops priced, a little uncertainly, in the mid hundreds. Certainly a bargain if they were real, but I wouldn't give five dollars for one.

There are some very skillful map reproductions around. Woodblock printed maps are the easiest to fake if one is trying to produce a forgery and indeed, we know of several very old world maps that have forged counterparts. There is a fake Reisch world that is making the rounds, and there are several Münster Americas fakes currently on the market. There are a few Matthew Seutter maps that were copied. The Seutters are most curious because they were done by means of copperplate engravings and printed on laid paper, and it is quite possible that they were not intended to deceive. The original maps are still not very valuable, they sell in the thousand dollar range even today and the elaborate forgeries appear to have been hardly worth the effort. I've not seen many of them, and they all appear to have been done some time ago, possibly as a series of legitimate reproductions and not intended to be passed off as originals.

There are some great fakes in modern history. The Thomas Wise forgeries are particularly well known and caused no end of embarrassment and financial distress as knowledge of them emerged. More recent were the Mormon forgeries. This involved a large number of manuscripts, letters and documents involving the early history of the Mormon church that were "found" and sold to the Church in the past few decades. A truly bizarre case, this one involved murder, scandal and some very important players. At least one culprit has been unmasked and he is now serving time in the Big House. Perhaps less well known, but more far reaching, is the growing awareness that many broadsides, especially those having to do with early Texas history are forgeries. The fakes began appearing a few years ago. Many appeared first at auction, some in inventories of private dealers. Many found their way into collections that were later donated to institutions. This latter circumstance raises a peculiar problem that makes the simple purchase of a fake broadside, and the attendant loss of a few hundred dollars pale by comparison. Let us invent a scenario. Sam Sixgun, Texas businessman builds a large collection of old deeds, Texas maps, broadsheets, proclamations and manuscripts. He is particularly proud of the large number of unique broadsides. He decides to donate them to his Alma Mater, Texas College, which is very pleased to accept. Sam Sixgun has the auction house from which he bought many of the items prepare an appraisal so that he can take the appropriate IRS deduction. He gets the appraisal, and Texas College gets the collection. The deduction of 1.5 million dollars, based on the appraisal, is reviewed routinely by the IRS and found to be appropriate. Sam Sixgun is an honest man who bought well through legitimate auction houses and Texas dealers and his donation makes a major contribution to an archive of Texas history. Now, along comes Suzie Scholar who has discovered that most of the broadsides are fakes and can demonstrate the fact. She has written a definitive work on the subject and a national scandal is brewing. Suddenly Sam Sixgun's donation is all hat and no cattle. Sam's deduction is questioned by the IRS who have now ascertained that the worthless fakes constituted two thirds of the donation and Sam now owes five years back taxes on over a million bucks. The auction house that made the appraisal is incorporated and has no assets. Texas College, embarrassed by the fiasco and embarrassed by the glossy catalogue it issued to inaugurate the collection doesn't want to know Sam, it simply wants to distance itself from the tainted goods. Sam, now in a nursing home, is in deep weeds all around. The lawyers will feed well on this one.

F.J. Manasek

The late Johnny Jenkins was a very prominent Americana dealer. A native Texan, he specialized in Texas material, had a thriving business and was respected worldwide. Johnny would always have a few wonderful early Texas broadsides in his inventory and major collectors were impressed with his ability to come up with some very rare items. Johnny also was a world class poker player. A few years ago Johnny's body was found floating in a ditch, a bullet in his head. His Mercedes was parked nearby. I think his death was ruled a suicide.

Chapter 7

London shop

Quaint old bookshops with shelves filled with ancient and valuable books. Shops stuffed with old prints and maps. Proprietors who really don't know, or care, just how much their goods are worth and are willing to sell them to anyone with American dollars. Very cheaply. Besides, there's so much more where that came from.

This view of London is one that I've heard quite often. Sometimes less emphatically, sometimes even more so.

The fabled riches of London is but another legend of the likes of El Dorado, the elephants' graveyard, or Prester John. But surely, such a place must exist. Where else would I get old maps? And why else would they be so expensive in my shop if I hadn't bought them somewhere else and just "jacked up the price?" The latter is one of the more irksome observations that visitors to my shop used to make with regularity. It's the London variant of the more general "Where do you get your stock?" question.

The London variant is asked principally by people who, at one time in their lives, have set foot outside this country and are therefore experts in the world's markets. Their London tour bus might have taken them past Foyle's or, if it was a tour for the well-read set, past the old Francis Edwards

F.J. Manasek

building on Marlebone High Street. "Aha!" they now think. "So this is where this guy buys his stuff." The corollary is, of course, the crafty realization that all they need to do is go to Foyles (or Zwemmer's, or the generic Ye Olde Mappe Shoppe) and buy the same things I have and save gobs of money. Once this realization sweeps over them like the Holy Spirit all is lost. Oxen and wainrope could not then drag them to the sales counter in this shop.

I've done the experiment. A few years ago a couple spent some delightful hours in my shop looking at old maps. They were pleased with what they saw, appreciated my explanations and were about to buy a very nice Blaeu Americas. The map was in wonderful condition, good wide margins and had splendid original hand color. Price, as I now recall, was about $5000. Then Enlightenment struck, and they knew with absolute certainty that they could buy this thing for a pittance and a song somewhere in London. The deal was off.

"We might be going to England next summer," he said. "We'll buy it there. It will be much cheaper."

Time to test my hypothesis. I had another copy of the same map in a lower drawer. I pulled it out and showed it to them. The map was equal to the first in all respects. "This one," I said, "I can sell for three thousand." Of course, my fingers were crossed, hoping that my theory was right and that they wouldn't take me up on the offer. Had they done so I would have lost money.

"No, we'll just buy our maps in London this summer and save some money."

Even people who really do know better can not quite silence that irksome little voice that tells them where I get all the deals. It isn't only maps. I think everything is viewed the same way.

Paleography is a personal interest of mine. There isn't much of a market for the stuff, but over the years I've accumulated some wonderful items and indeed, our depth in

70

Uncommon Value

some areas is quite good. A very decorative and interesting manuscript item that I try to have in stock is a peculiar type of Buddhist ordination text, extracted from the Pali Vinya. This text, called a Kammavaca, is written on rectangular sheets of lacquer in a thick, black text called Pali. Each page is a sheet of lacquer that has as a matrix a piece of the discarded robes of an older Buddhist monk. Lacquer is built up, and the brilliant red color is offset by gold, laid down in intricate designs. Over all this, the thick, rich brownish-black lacquer Pali text is written. Complete Kammavacas, consisting of 14 lacquer leaves and two wooden decorated covers can be quite expensive. The last one I sold was over a thousand dollars. I buy incomplete ones also, and salvage the individual leaves. They are sufficiently beautiful to find a ready market. I have seen them strung them together with nylon monofilament fishing line, much like a Venetian blind. When hung on a white wall, the red/gold/black ladderlike construction is spectacular. Curious individuals will buy individual leaves just because they are 'neat.' Thus, there is a regular, albeit very small, market that I have established for these things, and we have regular clients for them.

A few years ago, at a New York book fair, I was visited by a couple who seemed interested in my Kammavaca leaves.

"Where did you buy these?"

Resisting Tony Raimo's "garage sales" answer, I gave my own generic non-informative response. "We've been in business a long time. Things often come to us."

"We were in Paris last summer."

"Oh, goodie," was my thought, but my verbal response left off the 'goodie'.

"I saw some of these in a shop there. Did you buy them in Paris?"

"Nope."

"They must be very popular. They're all over!"

F.J. Manasek

Anyway, the whole world isn't discernible to all. Nor can one world be explained to those who inhabit another. President Jimmy Carter really believed that the world was just like Plains Georgia, but only bigger. If you knew Plains, you had it knocked. We all know where that concept got him. I knew a woman, now in her eighties, who is from a North German immigrant family. Her father was an Evangelical Lutheran minister in a small midwestern town, having emigrated with his flock. This woman, as a result of her restricted world view, hates the East Coast, people of South German stock, but also Catholics, Jews, New Yorkers and Harvard as well as anything else that is not a simple iteration of her known world. A similar phenomenon may also explain why relatively few younger people collect older books and maps. Expense aside, very old books and maps are outside their known world and modern education does not provide a sound enough intellectual platform from which to reach out to things unfamiliar.

I used to try to explain to people that I have multiple sources, that it's a network, that I buy from people who trust me and so on. Yes, I do buy in London but I also sell more there than I buy. Disbelief. Yes, I buy in Germany, but I also sell more than I buy. Disbelief. No, I don't buy much in Paris. Too expensive. Disbelief. Foreign dealers, I would patiently explain, came here to buy. Exchange rates. More stuff here. Disbelief. We all know London is the place to buy.

I finally saw the light.

I'll open a shop in London. If everyone and his brother thinks things are dirt cheap in London, why should I fight it. I'm sure Mao had something to say about going with the flow. Willow bend with wind. Willow grow big. Oak snap over. Something like that.

The timing seemed right. My son was going off to college and I had no other real personal obligations in the States. My business in Hanover could stand my absence for periods of time. The economy seemed to be doing well, and

Uncommon Value

the London dealers were all showing evidence of prosperity. The tourist trade was booming. Americans were still flocking to London in droves as well as in airplanes. And Americans accounted for most of map sales in London. Surprising as it may seem, in the antiques trade at that time something well over half of all sales in England, perhaps as much as sixty percent of the market, depended upon American buyers. American dollars were the engine that drove that market. To a lesser extent the book trade was also dependent upon American buyers. I don't know how much of the English map trade depended upon American buyers, but it clearly was a substantial amount. One need only look at prices for maps of American interest compared to prices for similar maps of other parts of the world.

Bloomsbury was one of my favorite areas of London. For twenty years I have stayed there whenever I was in London. I had the great pleasure of introducing my son, Jared to London via Bloomsbury. Whenever I could, I would take him with me and thus, as a lad of about 8 years, Jared started learning about London with Bloomsbury as a home base.

Bloomsbury had a wonderful range of hotels and bed-and-breakfasts. All the little streets were lined with B&B's. Some of these B&B's as well as many modest hotels have since become rather pricey. The old Hotel Montague, on Montague Street certainly fell victim to the real estate boom of the eighties. Years ago it was a bit of a downscale place. It had a bar, called the Redwood Bar. So-called, because it had a huge slab of a redwood tree, showing growth rings, hanging on the wall. Fluorescent lights on the ceiling and uncomfortable plastic seats completed the decor. At closing, the bar was encircled by a meshwork screen. Now, the Montague could serve as a backdrop for Vogue. In the summer of '93 Anne and I had cocktails in the bar, no longer with a slab of redwood tree in evidence. Despite the glitz and sophisticated decor, the bartender still could not make a martini cocktail.

F.J. Manasek

For several years I used a small, run-down B&B that faced Bloomsbury Square as a London base. It was about as downscale as one can get and not be in a dangerous neighborhood. Some of my Dutch colleagues still stay there, preferring its proletarian ambiance to creature comfort. Being a B&B, it serves breakfast. In a dining room in the cellar, there are some tables and chairs where one can sit and be assaulted by surly kitchen staff who also take the orders. Bacon and eggs, ham and eggs, cold cereal, coffee and tea are the fare. Everything, except the cereal and beverage is cooked (or brought to room temperature) in grease. Jared and I decided that they cooked the weeks' eggs on Wednesdays. We re-christianed the place the "Barfing Arms" as a tribute to the skills of the kitchen staff. I recall once telling my friend Ronald Singer, a Chicagoan, née South African, about the place. Ron, a very urbane and international character was someone who knew London quite well, certainly better than I. When I mentioned that we stayed at the Barfing Arms, Ron looked puzzled. "I'm afraid I don't know the Barfing," he admitted. But others must have. My sister, Marlene, also heard me call it the Barfing. Once, when I was staying there for some length of time she wrote me a letter, addressed to me, care of the Barfing Arms. It arrived.

The Barfing was home, I'm quite convinced, to the CIA. Quite often there were very freshly scrubbed faces in the breakfast crowd. Clean healthy American faces, Moonie-like in their simple adoration of the True Faith. I used to make a point of sitting at their tables if there was space. It was fun listening to them. "Hi! I'm Joe Shmoe! I'm visiting London! I work for the Army! I used to live in Iowa! I live in Reston Virginia! I'm over on vacation!" What other company has employees who talk like assholes all the time? I did the experiment once. I looked up from my plate of Wednesday eggs and grease, raised an eyebrow and very quietly asked, "Company taking care of you?"

Bloomsbury is wonderful for many other reasons. It is a truly socially integrated area. Bums and millionaires walk the same streets. Bloomsbury Square is a typical little London square with benches where people sit and chat, grassy knolls where children play and bushes where bums sleep it off. Only once have I ever seen violence in Bloomsbury. That was the time a bum chased an American and his wife into the druggist's. The little shop, next to Alan Alan's Magic Spot on Southampton Row (Alan Alan is now retired and the druggist has expanded into his space) could barely contain the large American, his large wife and me. I was in the shop buying blackcurrant pastilles. (I am addicted to blackcurrant pastilles, Jared is addicted to them, as is Anne.) "I'll kill the asshole!" announced the Large American. Meanwhile, the bum was standing on the sidewalk daring the Large American to come out. The bum had taken off his shirt and was posing, bare-chested and boxer-like, on the sidewalk. "I'll kill the asshole!" said the American, whose accent by now had clearly revealed him as a Texan. The Texan looked at me. "I'll kill the asshole."

Bloomsbury used to have a good representation in the antiquarian bookselling world. However, the 70's and 80's witnessed an eclipse of this activity. Of all the venerable names, only Louis Bondy remained (alas, Louis Bondy died last year, a book dealer to the end). Some newcomers did move in following the urban renewal of the early 80's but the flavor was never the same. The early 80's were a potentially profitable time for Bloomsbury real estate. The dollar was almost equal to a pound sterling and the byways of Bloomsbury were filled with buildings that had suffered over time. Many of them had not been renovated since before the war and their time was up. There was talk of turning Museum Street into a pedestrian mall; talk of expanding the British Museum southward; talk, talk, talk. I found a wonderful building that was located perfectly, just the right size and quite cheap. If you had had the chance to buy a building in New York less than a block from the American Museum of Natural History, or less than a block from the Metropolitan Museum for around $100,000. (yes, it was a fixer upper) would you have done it? My accountant, a

F.J. Manasek

Midwesterner, advised me against it. In retrospect, I don't think he knew where London was. I didn't buy the building, but a few years later did get space on the same street.

Cartographia Ltd. was a very well respected firm of London antiquarian mapsellers. Dealing from space near Covent Garden, the Marsdens built quite a nice business. Bloomsbury urban renewal created some very attractive space in newly renovated buildings. An old courtyard, largely filled with building rubble, had been cleared, renovated and gentrified. Pied Bull Yard, on Bury Place now had a wine bar, a dealer in paintings, a dealer in antique cameras, a dealer in modern first editions and the newly moved Cartographia Ltd. This was also the time when London rents jumped skyhigh. The economy was booming and optimism grew like weeds in every sidewalk crack. Business owners signed leases without regard for tomorrow.

Leases, in England, are quite different than they are in the States. If I sign a lease in England with a landlord, say for 50 years, I have the right to sell that lease to someone else. The landlord has the right to increase the rent by means of periodic rent reviews. So far, so good. I'm now 20 years into the lease and having made my fortune selling souvenirs to the tourist, I retire to my cottage near Bath. I have sold my shop and the lease to someone else who, some 10 years later loses his shirt at the track and goes bankrupt. He skips town and doesn't pay the rent for a year or so. The rent, meanwhile has increased by means of the periodic rent review and is now staggeringly high. The landlord can't find the bloke, but can find me. Under English law, I am responsible for all the unpaid rent (at the new rates), interest and the lease is mine again. For the remaining 20 years. Clearly one needs a cool head and a good solicitor when entering into a lease in England.

The Cartographia Ltd. shop in Pied Bull Yard was large, spacious and a block too far from the Museum traffic. Kit Marsden took in boarders to help pay the rent. One of the boarders was Peter Griffiths, a very knowledgeable rare

Uncommon Value

bookseller doing business as Vanbrugh Rare Books. Peter, a short, pudgy pleasant fellow built a thriving little business in a corner of the Cartographia Ltd. space. He produced a fine catalogue that listed some wonderful old books at decent prices. He had a good American trade and had a good institutional client base. Although Peter lacked capital for expansion, he signed a lease for a shop in a newly renovated building a block away on Museum Street.

Peter and I had made some mutually satisfactory transactions. He sold for me a wonderful old book on alchemy that bore the arms of the Wizard Earle deeply embossed with gold on the vellum binding. It was a book that I had bought at a fair in California for a few hundred dollars and Peter sold it for me for over a thousand pounds. I found a good vellum binding (empty) from a Blaeu atlas from 1650 that Peter needed to complete the repairs to some books he had. I bought a very nice Shakespeare Fourth Folio from Peter. And so it went. Many mutually satisfactory transactions.

Peter had concerns about cash flow in his new shop and was quite willing to sublet space to me. I mentioned this to several of my friends in the London book and mapselling trade. Most mapsellers had not heard of him, the booksellers were quite noncommittal. Only one made some sort of negative noise which I did not follow through on. I suppose I didn't want to jeopardize the deal, so I didn't pursue the reason for the less than positive response. I really wanted space on Museum Street, WC1.

Museum Street was the perfect place for an upscale map gallery and rare book shop. David Pritchard-Jones had a great shop on the street; he sold general old books and was very knowledgeable. Ulysses, sellers of antiquarian travel books were on the street as were a paintings gallery and a printshop. All within a block of the British Museum, merely a few doors from the building I had wanted to buy only a few years earlier. A couple of nice cafes, a dealer in Japanese antiquities, a stationer's and a food shop filled the rest of the street. Of course, the Museum Pub was on the corner closest to the BM and the Plough just across the street from our new shop.

The Plough was a splendid pub. The Plough referred, of course, to the constellation of The Plough, known more commonly as the Great Bear or Ursa Major or the Big Dipper. The Brits call the asterism of the Big Dipper The Plough, and the pub by that name had for years a wonderful outdoor hanging sign with the constellation on it. I loved that dark green sign with the golden stars, and would make a point of looking at it each time I was in Bloomsbury. Sometime in the 80's The Plough changed hands and the new owner probably had not God's own idea why a pub called the Plough should have stars on its sign. The old stellar sign disappeared and in its stead was hung a new sign, showing a horse pulling a plow! Civilization is not in decline, it's in a rout.

Peter's shop plans progressed rapidly and as soon as the building renovations were completed we dealt with the interior space. Mahogany bookshelves lined the walls, the floor was a burnt pine, we put down several oriental carpets and brought in some very nice desks and tables. I put in a few bins for maps and began moving in some inventory. We opened in the early winter, a gloomy time but one full of promise. Unfortunately, just as we opened, the Gulf War began. Little did we realize that the Great Depression had started also. Business was, despite the circumstances, quite good. The location was super and the place looked fine. It embodied everyone's fantasy of what a rare bookshop should look like. Straight out of central casting.

My business in the States was prospering and I was looking forward to expanding the London operation. I planned to move all of the firm's science and medicine books to London where I felt there was a better market. I began packing about a thousand rare books for transshipment to London.

Uncommon Value

A shop in London serves two functions. One is selling. The other is buying. London supports a host of individuals called runners who earn their living carrying things from shop to shop and selling them. Many of them rummage through tips and dustbins, others go to flea markets, still others are known well enough to be able to take things from one shop, run across town and offer the good to another dealer. Although largely an underground economy (you don't give runners checks.) runners are an important source of inventory for many of London's fine book, map and print shops. Word was out among the runners that there was an American on Museum Street and they flocked to me in droves. In England, 'American' is often code for 'rich American'. Nonetheless, I bought very well and got some very nice things for inventory from the runners who befriended me. This source seemed to be cyclical, however. Buying was very good when I was there; when I went back to the States it dried up.

Meanwhile, Peter was running low on operating funds. The business seemed to be going well and it looked to me to be a temporary cash flow problem. I advanced him £20,000. By this time the Gulf War was going full tilt and the Great Depression had set in and my books were in London and Peter had my twenty thousand quid. Peter had taken in a large lot of wine books on consignment. They were good quality and sold steadily. One day I came into the shop and noticed they were all gone. Thinking they had been sold, I was glad for Peter's good fortune, but I soon learned that the consignor had angrily removed them all.

By July I realized that things were not going to get better and that the shop would not survive. Worse, I was afraid that my hard-won reputation was going to be destroyed unless I was very careful and intervened personally. I made certain that any debts incurred by me or on my behalf were paid promptly and that payment was made directly by me.

Cartographia Ltd., meanwhile, had suffered greatly. The depression had grown worse in England and many London shops were closing. Real estate prices were in free fall and everything was heading down except rents. Kit Marsden, director of Cartographia Ltd. finally folded the firm and quit the business. He had, in the interim, sublet space to John Forster. John expanded his antique barometer business into the space vacated by Peter Griffiths when he took Vanbrugh Rare Books to Museum St.

Forster took over the entire space in the Pied Bull Yard shop and again expanded his barometer business, Barometer Faire, to fill the new space. Marsden had abandoned the remnants of his map business and the place was congested with huge plan chests filled with unsalable maps. The sorts of maps that accumulate slowly year in and year out despite one's best efforts to keep them out of inventory. It doesn't matter how cheaply one prices them. They don't sell.

John is a scrupulously honest and decent fellow and we always got along. He had been following Peter's activities with some bemusement, but sympathized with me in my plight. I proposed to John that I move my business in with his. We struck a deal, shook hands and I had new premises. It took two days to move my books and maps over from Museum St., but at least they now were safe.

Peter still owed me £20,000. Actually somewhat less, since I had been deducting rent from the balance due me. Nonetheless, I despaired of ever seeing it again. Peter deftly sidestepped all discussion and whenever I brought up the subject it was turned aside with charm and aplomb.

One day, when the shop was empty save for the secretary, and Peter was sitting alone at his desk, I asked him to come outside with me. We stood on the sidewalk in a light London drizzle and Peter again told me he couldn't pay. "Frank," he said in his most earnest, "Frank, I want to pay you but you know how bad business is. I don't have the money."

"That doesn't matter — I want it anyway." We went back and forth like this for a while, getting nowhere. I finally took a different tack. "Peter," I said, "I'm not going to take you to court — that's a waste of time and money. But you will pay me. That is not a discussable item. I want to be paid today. Don't forget, Peter, I'm from the States and we know how to deal with this sort of thing. I'm not very pleasant when pushed and you're pushing me." I'm not sure what this all meant, it was certainly not a threat — I had no intention of giving him a pair of cement shoes, but Peter didn't know that. He opted for prudence. That afternoon I got paid.

Peter continued to send out very attractive catalogues. They contained good books fairly priced and he did well by all accounts. I have always though he had a good book sense and was able to sell very well into the American market. However, some time in 1993 he sent a letter to all American recipients of his catalogue asking for a donation of, I think, $20.00 each to "keep London's only (sic) antiquarian bookshop in business." I don't know how well his appeal did, but the next I heard was that he had taken all his books out of the shop one weekend and disappeared. The CID was now looking for him, he was officially a missing person and a lot of unhappy dealers were looking for him also. I hope the CID find him before the dealers do. Peter caused me and a lot of other people a lot of grief, but I do not think he is evil. He's more like Captain Hook, and I wish him well.

I think the rare book and map market has changed more in the past two or three years than in the previous twenty. For generations London had dominated and its dealers had grown fat. The recession of the early 1990's, a depression in parts of London, had taken its toll. I recall standing on the sidewalk in St. James very early one Sunday morning with Desmond Burgess, the very private and very knowledgeable London dealer. Desmond pointed at all the prosperous looking buildings, including a bank building across the street. "All these buildings are empty," he said. "They all have occupants, but they are just for show. The landlords don't want the buildings to look empty so they allow businesses to use them." I think what was happening was that landlords didn't want to write leases at a lower rate because the value of a commercial property is related to its rental value. If they acknowledged that rents had gone down, then the book value of the building would go down and the banks would call in the loan and the whole real estate bubble would pop. With a major part of London's capitol tied up in devalued real estate, it is no wonder that the antiques market, including books and maps was soft.

John Forster and I continued the business, reincarnated as "Cartographia London." We issued catalogues, did fairs and generally did well. John continued his barometer business and I strengthened the map side of the endeavor. My hypothesis proved correct. I sold a lot of maps at prices far higher than I could have gotten in the States. Most people just assumed that London prices were lower and did not even question them. Nor did they question me. Many times American visitors to the shop on Bury Place assumed that I was a Brit, even after spending time talking with me. People hear what they want to hear, or what they expect. I never tried to affect an English accent, although they are dynamite when selling to Americans. There's a husband and wife team of American map dealers who work the midwestern antiques shows. Neither of them have any claim to Britain, yet he ever so slightly puts on what he thinks is a British accent. It works wonders, especially in the hinterland.

I had a wonderful time working with John and his American wife, Marlene. We put in long hours and were actually doing a bit more than treading water during all those dreadful months of the long English depression. However, the times conspired against us. Not only were we in the grips of a national recession, but London itself was losing its preeminence as a center for map and bookselling. We were solvent but it wasn't worth the effort. John decided to pack it in and Cartographia London, née Cartographia Ltd. finally died. I took the best pieces of my inventory back to Hanover and auctioned off the rest. John and Marlene moved to the States and London was minus a very nice shop.

Uncommon Value

Despite the vicissitudes of the national economy, Peter Griffiths and the long commutes, I look back on my London experience with great pleasure. I shall always be thankful for the kindness of the great people in the Bloomsbury trade, the good discussions I had with Robert Frew and Ian Mackenzie, who had that great bookshop down the street from the British Museum, David Pritchard-Jones who had a shop across the street and the innumerable runners with whom I had lagers in the Plough, traded pounds for maps, gossiped and lied about our great finds.

The shop in Pied Bull Yard is still empty but the old sign is still in the window braving time and defying change. There have been a few business failures on the block, the little supermarket is gone but the cafe is still there and the espresso is as good as ever and the smile that greets me as genuine as before.

Bloomsbury is still my London home although I no longer stay at the Barfing. Anne has been adopted by Bloomsbury and we both look forward to our stays there. What pleasure it is to arrive after a long flight from somewhere foreign, walk up from the Holburn tube stop to our hotel and be welcomed home!

Chapter 8

West to the East

Sometime in the mid seventies I began to do a lot of business with Japan. Much of it was with woodblock prints, scrolls, and printed books. I also became fascinated with Japanese woodblock printed maps and with the help of my colleague, Atsuyo Nakamura, bought and sold hundreds of them. I think we were the largest Western dealers in woodblock maps for many years. My trips back and forth became more frequent and I lived there for a short while.

Japan hit me right between the eyes. Today, more than twenty years after my first trip to Japan, I can still relive that fantastic experience that was my first visit. I think it was December 1974, the winter of my first trip to Mars. I landed at the old international airport, Hanada (meaning, literally, winged rice-field), and took the monorail into Tokyo. I don't recall, after some 20 years, where the monorail left me off, but I took a taxi from there to my hotel in Akasaka, the Hotel New Japan. The New Japan was one of the first new post-war hotels to be built in Tokyo, but was already in a noticeable state of decline. I liked it immediately, adopted it and stayed there whenever I was in Tokyo for years to come. It later burned with a tragic loss of life.

Uncommon Value

Tokyo was a city filled with wondrous things. The Kanda, the old bookseller's district just north of the Imperial Palace had many shops, some very famous and others not so famous. I was particularly impressed by the large numbers of woodblock printed picture books that were everywhere. These small books, each pair of folded pages printed from a single carved woodblock, represented some of the finest book art anywhere. And here were stacks of them.

Many of the dealers in woodblock prints were still unused to the international scene and were insulated from many of the market forces that controlled the prices of prints outside of Japan. I recall buying three copies of one of Yoshida's nudes. That print had just sold, as I recall, for about $800. at Sotheby's. It cost me just under $100. in Tokyo.

There are many other such examples of price disparities, but most apparent to me was a peculiar attitude among Japanese regarding their major graphic art form, the woodblock print. There are many masters in this medium, acknowledged as such worldwide. We all recognize the names of Utamaro, Haronobu, Hiroshige just to name a few. These produced brilliant images during the 18th and 19th centuries. Interestingly, the artists did not cut their own blocks; rather they were associated with different publishers who hired block cutters to do the carving and then had separate printers to print the image. Unlike in the West, where the artist held more control over the entire process, the Japanese system inserted many individuals between artist and image.

In addition to the masters of world fame, Japan produced many artists of lesser quality. Some of them, such as Toyokuni III, were incredibly prolific. He had a huge outpouring of prints, sort of the Leonard Baskin of Ukiyo-e. I found that most of the images by these individuals were ridiculously cheap. And yet, continuing with Toyokuni III as an example, they produced some spectacular images. Indeed, much of what they produced was of minor quality, but they

F.J. Manasek

achieved brilliance at times. The Japanese didn't seem to make distinctions between the quality of these artist's images, but lumped them all together in the dross category. They had two things going for them; they were prolific and they were undercollected. I recall seeing stacks of oban sized woodblock prints, each stack several feet high. Each print priced at a few dollars. It didn't take me long to fill a suitcase. Several other American dealers also traveled to Japan a few times a year to stock up. One, owner of a prominent New York gallery used to tell her clients in the States that she never bought in Japan. "Too expensive. We only buy in America." She bought armloads in Japan and if I got there shortly after she had gone through I would have slim pickings, indeed.

Tokyo is quite a pleasant city. It has a good underground, and to anyone used to New York City subways and rush hours, the Tokyo rushawa is rather mild. There weren't any very tall buildings, presumably because of the earthquake danger, so the population density of even the downtown business districts was quite low — nothing like the thousands of people pouring out of New York skyscrapers at quitting time. The city is really a large accretion of small towns that had just sort of grown contiguous. Many of these little areas were superficially much alike and I had the impression of Tokyo as a virus with endlessly repeating surface coat subunits. And endless, it does seem.

After a day's exploring and buying, I would return to the New Japan and my adopted area of Akasaka. Akasaka was, to me, sort of my Japanese Bloomsbury. It had soul and heart. Akasaka had still some of the few remaining true geisha, and in the grand tradition, the geisha were transported to their destinations in tiny jinrikshaws, canopy up and isinglas side-curtains closed. Two or three of these vehicles were parked by day in a small parking lot and a few times I saw them clatter down the street at night. The glitter and glitz of the narrow streets of Akasaka at night, lighted by

Uncommon Value

hundreds of neon signs, all unintelligible to me, was simply wonderful.

There were a few antique shops on the outskirts of Akasaka. I would frequent these and buy the odd items that fitted into my own inventory. I did indeed buy some wondrous things from these little shops. I once got a complete set of woodblock printed district maps of Edo (the old name for Tokyo). Done in the waning days of the Shogunate, the maps dated from between 1840 and 1855 and were in fine (increasingly called 'mint') condition. I think the whole set cost less than fifty dollars.

One of the dealers had a few fabric stencils on display. Many Japanese fabrics had dyed designs. These designs were applied by means of stencils, using the dye-resist method. Unlike direct stenciling, in dye-resist, one paints a substance called a resist through the stencil. The resist is so called since it resists dye. Thus, wherever there is resist, the fabric "resists" dye and remains uncolored. In classical Japanese stenciling, the resist was a form of wheat paste. The stencils themselves were masterworks of design and execution. Made of two sheets of heavy paper, the stencils had often very elaborate motifs requiring extremely delicate cutting and required support for the thin tendrils of paper left floating in the design. This support came from hair that was embedded between the papers, spiderweb-like. The entire stencil and hair sandwich was sized with persimmon juice, giving it a deep, venous blood color. I inquired about the stencils on display. By this time I had a reasonably good Japanese vocabulary that I could string into simple sentences. The dealer, I learned, had a warehouse full of these stencils.

I bought the lot. In the best tradition of the marketplace, this was a real deal. The Japanese dealer thought that he had taken the gaijin for a walk around the block. I, in turn, knew that I had bested the Tokyo dealer. We were both very pleased. I sold three thousand of those stencils to a museum. I still have the rest and they continue to sell, albeit less dramatically. My supply will last into the next generation, but my profits have already been more than satisfactory.

One heard, and still hears, horror stories about the cost of food in Japan. Two hundred dollar melons. Five hundred dollar meals. This is the stuff that news is made of. If you're NBC. These melons are indeed very expensive, but the newscasters never tell you (they probably don't know) that they are a very special ceremonial or gift melon, grown specially so that the stem has the correct angle; they are packed in a special straw in a special wooden box and are given as special gifts. Very significant. If you go into a local shop, you can buy a normal melon for not too much more than they cost in big city downtowns here. I used to eat in Chinese restaurants. These are generally little places that have, in their windows, wax models of the food they serve. In the late 70's, a nice lunch cost about ¥400, or a buck and a quarter. The two great fictions about Japan, the rushawa crowds and the cost of meals were obviously invented by retired ministers' wives from Peoria who had never seen the New York or Paris underground and who had never eaten anywhere other than their hotel dining rooms the one time they were in Tokyo on a church tour. It makes good copy, so the news media perpetuate the fiction.

My son, Jared, used to accompany me whenever possible. At that time, he was enrolled in a private school in Chicago and I could readily get permission for him to miss class so that he could visit Japan. Whenever he did this, I would take his class work with us and he would have to spend part of each day working in our hotel room on his class assignments. In addition, he was always expected to give a slide talk to his class on his return. On the whole, I think he learned a lot more by traveling with me than had he stayed in Chicago. Fortunately his school thought so also and they cooperated in making his frequent trips not only possible, but good learning experiences by expecting him to assemble some sort of formal and coherent results. Jared, even as an eight year old lad, had his favorite restaurants in

Uncommon Value

Tokyo. He loved the Korean Barbecue in Akasaka. We ate there quite often.

I usually spent a week or so in Tokyo, which is about how long it took to visit my contacts and leave a bit of time to try to establish new ones. This also left some time to play. My next stop was usually Kyoto. Both Jared and I liked to travel on the Shinkansen, or bullet train, which we took from Tokyo to Kyoto.

For several years I stayed in a Japanese style inn, a ryokan, when I was in Kyoto. Somehow, this seemed appropriate when visiting that wonderful old imperial city. "My" ryokan was the Hayama Ryokan, a very small place off Higashi-oji dori. The Hayama had about six private rooms overlooking a small garden, dank with moss and lantern stones. Higashi-oji dori is a busy street on the East side of Kyoto. Traffic roars all day; there are no sidewalks, just some low mobile curbs affording pedestrians some two feet or so of semi-private walkways along the building facades. A wonderful street, the starting point for going to Kiyo-misu; passing just a block or so from the Yasaka Pagoda, going north to Kyoto University and bustling with life all along its path. I have a small five-panel woodblock print from the 17th century showing Kyoto along this street. I treasure it; it shows the Yasaka Pagoda and from there I can point to where the Hayama Ryokan should have been on this print. It has captured a flavor of the region that is there today.

Traditional Japanese breakfast is served in Hayama Ryokan. Includes raw egg on miso soup. Rice, seaweed, tea. I have many fond memories of staying here. The last time was with two very good friends, Isaac Harary from Los Angeles and Radovan Zak from Chicago. We sat for hours on the tatami floor and laughed, told stories and drank beer.

It was a bit difficult to do business from the Hayama Ryokan, especially as I had to pack lots of things for shipping. I found it more convenient to stay in a western style hotel and never returned to the Hayama Ryokan. I walked past it several times since, always remembering its hospitality, good friends, laughter and beer.

I finally settled on, horrors of horrors, the Holiday Inn as a Kyoto base. Horiday Inn Hoteru, as taxi-drivers called it, was located in the northeast corner of the city. Jared and I could walk out to the bamboo groves with ease. It was also on the trolley line, before they took out the trolley line. Moreover, it was one of the cheapest places to stay and the bartender could make decent martinis.

In all but the sweltering days of July, I walked from the Holiday Inn to the center of town, where I would meet with the private dealers. Scrolls, screens and woodblock prints were examined, picked, bargained over and bought. I was particularly fortunate in buying, once, a very large collection of kacho-ga or natural history paintings. Birds, flowers, bugs. Hundreds of them, creating somewhat of a shipping problem since they were too heavy for me to carry home.

Kyoto also had several shops loaded with ehon, the Japanese woodblock printed books of which I'm so fond. Over the years I must have bought hundreds of them in Kyoto. They are light, and I usually packed them into suitcases. Carefully catalogued, they did very well and several institutions became my very good clients. I was also dealing in more esoteric things. There was a wonderful shop in Kyoto that was filled with manuscripts as well as very early calligraphy and printing. The owner's niece was one of the most beautiful young women I have ever seen anywhere in the world. Times like that made me wish I was twenty years younger and Japanese. I bought a beautiful Kamakura period e-maki Buddhist scroll there one year. I'm still sorry that I sold it. It was a wonderful work from the early 14th Century.

There are great restaurants in Kyoto, including little noodle shops and even smaller Chinese food eateries. I loved spending the late mornings looking around, inspecting prints and books and then having a nice lunch. I latched onto a very downscale sushi shop with a little endless conveyor belt carrying individual plates of sushi. Tea was piped throughout the restaurant through thin pipes. I think the cost was ¥150 per plate. I could easily go through ten plates per lunch, which in those days was still about five dollars. Evenings, Kappa's was perhaps my favorite Kyoto restaurant. There was indeed a Kappa who owned the place. It was a noisy, raucous restaurant with a large "U" shaped counter and some very small tables. Each time someone entered, the patrons would shout a welcome. The food was incredibly good, much of it was swimming about in tanks until just before it was prepared. Smoky, noisy, filled with laughter.

Laughter fills Japan. Life is full of humor and much of this can be seen in old paintings and prints. We need only look at the Meiji period woodblock prints of Tamenobu to see a keen perception of the humor of everyday life. I was reminded of this when, in a scroll-dealers, we were waiting out a sudden downpour. A woman had taken shelter underneath the dealer's awning, when suddenly she shrieked and ran out into the rainstorm, yelling and thrashing. I hadn't seen what had happened, and my Japanese wasn't good enough to understand what the dealer was trying to tell me, all the while laughing so hard he kept falling over. Seems there was a bird's nest under the awning. Thumbing rapidly through his English language dictionary the dealer explained. "Swarrow nest. Swarrow shit on woman head." Imagine had this happened in Switzerland. What would have been considered worse? Shitting or laughing?

By the time the 80's dawned, it was becoming more difficult to find bargains in Japan. Most of the dealers there were getting picked over by westerners and the pipelines were emptying. But there were other factors contributing to the drying up of good old material.

The Japanese, who had been insular for thousands of years, began looking outward. It is difficult for us Americans to realize how restrictive their culture was with regard to anything foreign. While there were no absolute legal restrictions on foreign travel, until rather recently a Japanese citizen's passport was valid for only one foreign destination or trip. As a Japanese, if you wanted to travel to France, for example, your passport was issued for that purpose. Too much foreign travel was frowned upon by the culture. Nothing explicit would ever be stated; there were no laws against it but society disapproved. That was the kiss of death. As Japanese companies became global powers, it became necessary to send their executives, engineers, technicians to all parts of the world. This kind of exposure and experience was important, as it is in every global endeavor, and Japanese executives who had foreign experience found that it helped their careers back with the company at home. Not, however, if they took to their global assignments with too much enthusiasm and overstayed the normal time period of a foreign assignment. I've been told that this was about three years. It was felt back home, that if one overstayed this time limit, some degree of "Japanese-ness" would be lost. People who did this found their careers damaged. American academia had a similar problem, but for different reasons. In the heyday of basic science research, some twenty or so years ago most young people with new degrees would spend a few years in a post-doctoral position. This was a delicious time in which a young person would have no teaching or administrative responsibility, no fund-raising responsibilities, just the opportunity to work very hard in a senior scientist's laboratory and produce a body of work to demonstrate potential. From a good post-doc in a good lab to a good faculty position was a smooth transition. If one did a post-doc in a foreign lab there might be problems. Not cultural ones. Half the people in American academia have foreign roots, accents or spouses. The problem here was one of mentoring. In the days of the old boy system, it was harder to get plugged into a good department in a first-rate University from a foreign post-doc because of connections, or lack of them. In Japan it was because of xenophobia.

The Japanese were remarkably homogeneous. For thousands of years they inbred, remained culturally isolated, importing only those things they wanted, and kept everything else out. I think there is a degree of unspoken communication among Japanese that is similar to the way any closely knit family anywhere in the world communicates over the dinner table. I have seen many complex deals go down. Many of these took a lot of time, but mostly quiet time, with the individuals nodding, sucking on their teeth, smiling or making minor statements. As an outsider, I had the feeling that what I was witnessing was thousands of years of common culture and goals being expressed by cues and signals unimaginable to us gaijin. We weren't part of the club. We could never be.

With the arrival of the American Black Ships under Perry, Japan was opened to the West. The Tokugawa Shogunate fell, but it had been on the edge of the precipice for some time. It was clear to the progressive elements in Japan that they were doomed if they did not co-opt those elements of the foreign cultures that could destroy them. This they did, creating an intriguing hybrid culture, retaining pure Japan at some level, but overlaying it with Western things, such as ironclads, cannon, railroads and telegraphs. Unfortunately, for a period of time the pendulum swung the other way and they embraced a lot of other western elements, at the expense of their own culture. Protestant missionaries flooded Japan. These were mostly ignorant, semi-educated louts who huckstered Jesus and fundamentalism. I can't help believe that some of these incursions helped lay the groundwork for later overt hostilities.

Japan is still a closed society. I often found it difficult to rent rooms in hotels other than in the major western-style ones. Many of the hotels used by Japanese businessmen are well located and convenient. They are also less expensive than the Hiltons, Okuras, and the Grand Hotels. But getting into them is another problem. Time after time I was told "Sorry, no room." I finally figured out how to do it. I would wait in the lobby until other guests came in, then I would get in line before them. If there was someone on line behind me, it was more difficult for the desk clerk to tell me there wasn't any room. Once or twice I had to wait until the Japanese behind me got a room to prove to the clerk that there was indeed space. Restaurants were another matter. Anyone can go into a small eatery or an average restaurant. The staff might not like it, but they never made a fuss. However, if any westerner tried to go to some of the great Japanese restaurants in any major city he'd find rather quickly that he was trying to drink from the 'white only' water fountain. This wasn't often a problem, since these restaurants are largely unknown to the gaijin, hence not troubled by such indiscretions. A few years ago some Japanese friends took me to one of the great restaurants of Japan. Located near Hamamatsu, the thatched-roofed restaurant overlooked one of the great gardens. Our meal took several wonderful hours. Judging by the distant curiosity I evoked, I must have been the first, or nearly so, Westerner to have eaten under those splendid old roofs. All went well and I didn't disgrace my hosts but I have no illusion that I could have come back alone. Huge segments of Japanese society and institutions are simply closed to non-Japanese. And most westerners don't even know it because of the language barrier and the enormous cultural gulf.

Nonetheless despite the persistent xenophobia, Japanese were beginning to assimilate information about foreigners. They became tourists. Like tourists everywhere, they went to museums and saw wonderful things. Among the wonderful things they saw were Japanese prints, scrolls, screens, books, pottery and manuscripts. Some of the major collections of these things are in the Western world. Some of the great collectors, scholars and dealers in these things are Western. Suddenly, or at least over a few decades, Japanese saw that the great artifacts of their culture were important in a universal human sense. Things that had had little value suddenly were seen in a very different light. Japanese began buying their own cultural artifacts in addition to the impressionists peddled by Christoby's.

Prosperity and a more global perception changed the way Japanese looked at themselves. No longer would there be piles of five-dollar Ukiyo-e prints, no longer would the wonderful 19th century scrolls be available in armloads. The Japanese were now buying them.

Sort of like a slow, giant molasses tidal wave, collectables move from one culture to another, often then turn around and go back. Japanese began buying back their own artifacts. American and European dealers were scrambling to acquire Japanese items for their profitable return home. This caused a minor boom in even lesser Japanese items in this country. Japanese were not buying rubbish. Big money was going after big items and they were not "buying everything Japanese in sight." Nonetheless, all a dealer had to do was smile knowingly when a buyer would broach this subject and it was assumed immediately that there were dozens of Japanese buyers in the wings, foaming. As soon as people thought that Japanese were buying something, those items would become more desirable. Remember, this is the time when the Japanese seemed to be invincible in the marketplace.

Of course they weren't invincible. The fact that Japanese tend to buy only through dealers with whom they have established relationships does tend to reduce the likelihood of getting bad deals but doesn't prevent it entirely. There was a fantastic episode some years ago that caused major upsets. A Japanese company decided to establish a private museum for ancient glass. They sent an emissary to London to buy items for their museum. He found enough ancient glass to fill the museum and then some. London, of course, is the center of such markets. All of the world's great museums go to London to buy. London dealers are the best in the world. What could possibly go wrong? Some years later it was discovered that every single item in the newly founded museum, now proudly showing its possessions in Tokyo, was fake. The dealer had returned to Iran and the hapless Japanese buyer committed suicide.

With their newly found internationalism Japanese began buying things they had virtually shunned only a few years earlier. Western maps of Japan, for example, always prized to some extent by western collectors, now had a vibrant new market. The beautiful 16th and 17th century maps by Ortelius, Blaeu, Jansson and the other great mapmakers of the golden age of Dutch cartography doubled in price. Just a few years earlier, it was virtually impossible to sell these maps at any price in Japan — there simply were too few collectors with the sophistication to see anything of value in any foreign item. Still, the Japanese market sought only the 'brand names' of foreign works. Regardless how good or attractive an item might be, if it wasn't by a great name it wasn't saleable. There was no middle market in collecting, suggesting that unlike in the West, the Japanese middle class had not yet discovered collecting. I've often heard it argued that this is because the small size of most Japanese dwellings precludes collecting. This argument might be valid if one is talking about collecting Edwardian sofas, but a world-class collection of prints can be stored in a single envelope. Half a million dollars in maps will fit into a small portfolio. My personal theory is that collecting is too individual an activity for Japanese. It is not a collective endeavor and requires the expression of individuality. Very uncomfortable, still, for the Japanese.

Japan also serves well as a good jumping off place for the rest of my Asian business. A relatively short flight gets me to Hong Kong. I stay on Kowloon for no particular reason other than I've always stayed there. It's just a short walk to the Star Ferry.

In Hong Kong I call on the few clients I have there, but mostly do the tourist things. Hong Kong is probably one of the world's great supermarkets for fake Chinese antiques. I am not sufficiently knowledgeable in the area of Chinese antiques to tell real from fake. Asian cultures have a different attitude about copying antiques and without getting into sophisticated analytic techniques there is no way some of them can be detected. I have occasionally found the old woodblock printed book, but never at really attractive prices. I have occasionally bought modern Chinese paintings here, but never remained impressed with them once I got them back home. I recall once buying about a dozen painted scrolls. After I had lived with them for a few weeks back in the States I could no longer understand why I had bought them in the first place. I finally took them to antique shows and sold them into the trade. Years later I still saw them, although by now they moved to other dealers and at very optimistic prices. I think these scrolls are probably still making the rounds in the trade.

Hong Kong is filled with all sorts of inferior copies of manufactured items. They are generally priced just enough below the real thing to make them appear worth it. I remember the suitcase I bought. I needed more space for the trip home and bought the cheapest suitcase I could find that I thought would survive the trip. It barely did, and only because I put a strap around it. It looked robust enough, but everything was fake. The chrome hardware was chrome plated plastic; the leather handle was cardboard with a leather veneer, and so on. They must have dumped thousands of these suitcases on unsuspecting tourists. Over the next year I saw at least a half dozen of them on baggage conveyors at airports all over the world, invariably in pieces, surrounded by their former contents. The things just came apart. Fortunately their half-life was short enough so that they disappeared from the face of the earth. It's been my impression that the baggage handlers in Madrid are about the most sadistic. What fun they must have had with these Hong Kong specials.

It wasn't only suitcases. The guy sitting next to me on the airplane leaving Hong Kong had just completed his first Asian holiday. I think he was newly retired. Obviously he was easily impressed, since the thing that had impressed him most about Hong Kong was a man on the street who had repaired his shoes. "Can you imagine, new heels in five minutes and for only about fifty cents? I tell you, these people are wonderful. So industrious." An hour into the flight, he returned from the toilet, limping and favoring his right foot. "Heel came off," he commented.

Chapter 9

Bangkok to Delhi

If a baseball bat had hit me in the back of my head, I don't think it would have been any more of a shock than my first sight of Bangkok. I had spent many years traveling through other parts of Asia before coming to Thailand. I had lived in Japan for a while and felt comfortable in the Asia I knew. Bangkok was one of those cities I had always wanted to visit; it was legendary for its beauty and charm.

Tired from a long air trip after a very busy business trip to Hong Kong, I taxied to my downtown hotel and slept. Next morning I got up to the most wonderful cacophony of every noise known to mechanized man. It was so loud that no individual sound was discernible; it was a curious roar of sound that had been put through the blender of Bangkok's streets. It seemed that every vehicle in the choked streets had straight exhaust pipes without benefit of muffler. Belching equal amounts of sound and blue odorous exhaust, the mass of vehicles created a pain to ear and nose, and after a while to eyes and lungs as well. The sound reverberated from one side of the street to the other and the blue exhaust simply filled the space and acted as ether for the transmission of the noise. It was June and the weather was hot. By early morning it was already about 90 degrees and humidity to match. The hot wet air was filled with blue exhaust smoke and ear splitting sound. And I couldn't speak a word of the language. The language is a sung one and I couldn't even hear the individual words.

As usual, in a new city, I start to wander about on foot. The heat, humidity and sound were almost unbearable, but the visual delights were more than compensation enough. Gilded temples with the most marvelous carvings. Long canoe-like boats on the waterways. An unbelievably beautiful people who were genuinely kind and helpful. It took me just a few hours to fall inextricably in love with Bangkok. I have never tired of this city and my love affair with it has grown with each visit.

Scattered throughout a number of districts are antique shops; some big, mostly small. While most of these shops traffic in fake genuine antiques, such as Buddha heads, they do have the occasional real item. I have for many years bought palm leaf books from Bangkok antique shops. These are books unlike the codex of the West. At first glance they look like Venetian blinds. Each leaf is made of a palm leaf that has been cut to size, dried and sized with milk. Text is incised with a needle which is sometimes heated. Carbon is sometimes rubbed into the incised leaf to make the writing more visible. Some of these leaves are decorated with wonderful images, but most of them are text devoid of other decoration. A 'book' might have several hundred leaves loosely strung on two cords that pass through wooden boards serving as top and bottom cover, thus the analogy to the Venetian blind. They were usually dirty, covered with ancient dust and releasing the characteristic smell of years in south-east Asian damp. If I find one of these books anywhere else in the world, be it in an American museum or in a German dealer's shop, I can tell if it came from here by taking a deep sniff of it. I don't think they ever lose the odor. A good nose is wonderful if trained properly. I can often tell if a map has had conservation and cleaning done to it by having a good smell, even when careful looking doesn't tell me. The smell of India is quite different, too. I used to be able to identify the Sundar Nagar market in Delhi as the place of origin by smell. It was quite different from other Indian markets, at least in terms of aroma. I recall once, in New York, buying manuscripts from an Indian dealer on the East Side. He was trying to tell me that they came from a great family. Maharajas and what-all. I inhaled them deeply, probably sucking in all sorts of spores, smiled at him and said "Sundar Nagar." The poor dealer blanched.

On my Bangkok book hunts, I would set out in the morning and wander from shop to shop and by early afternoon on a day with good hunting would have maybe six or eight good palm leaf books. Occasionally I would find wonderfully illustrated divination texts filled with arcane astrological symbols that covered the heavy khoi paper on which they were written. At the time I was buying these for a collector who was building one of the major private collections in this area. He still buys them, but it's become hard to find them splendid enough for his ever more discriminating taste.

I always seemed to get to South East Asia during the hot season when the temperature would get into the upper ninetys and the humidity would be there also. Sort of an exotic Baltimore. Despite the climatic similarity, I always preferred Bangkok to Baltimore. When I lived in Baltimore in the late 60's I would see the horizon red with flames from the burning city, as slash and burn cultural traits were being expressed. Even now, when I return to Baltimore I remember it as a city of heat and violence, whereas Bangkok is a city of heat, wonder and gentle culture.

After a day's work I always headed for the bar at the Oriental Hotel. A wonderful bar in a wonderful hotel. Rattan furniture. Potted palms. Ceiling fans. I always expected to see Sidney Greenstreet emerge from behind one of the potted plants. They served truly great martinis. Always a mark of a fine establishment. Veronica, who was often able to free herself and meet me in Bangkok was also a great fan of the Oriental Hotel. The hotel has one of the world's great

101

restaurants and those wonderful languid evenings by the river remain as some of our finer times together.

One of the many antique shops that populate Bangkok had a pile of unusually fine Tibetan tankas. These wonderfully painted images on cloth are filled with Buddhist iconography. Tankas and mandalas have within them images that respond to, and elicit, the deepest perceptions of humans of all cultures. There is a large Western literature on these images as symbols and the way people react to them, but relatively little has been written on the iconography itself. The meaning of the images, and the detail within them, in the context of the Buddhist belief system remains a mystery; I do not understand the symbols of the tanka, but respond to them in some primeval manner, a manner shared perhaps by all humans.

I bought the entire pile of tankas. Dating these things is difficult. The iconography is highly conserved and there is little difference between the images of 75 years ago and the images of 200 years ago. These images were very important to the Buddhism of Tibet and neither they nor the styles in which they were painted were permitted to change. Until recently. Tankas made for the tourist trade of today are easily spotted. It's as though I tried to copy a page of calligraphy by an ancient Chinese master. The tankas I bought were old and good. I sold them over the next several years to serious collectors. In addition, I was profoundly changed by them. Their images are very powerful. One of the finer specimens has remained with Veronica and graces her Paris flat. An old friend to greet us when when we both happen to be in Paris at the same time.

Bangkok has become the 'sex capitol of the world' or so some claim. I remember being there once on Buddha's birthday and the whorehouses were asked to remain closed out of respect for the Buddha. Out of respect for the Buddha, they opened an hour later than usual. Everyone has a sister for sale. I was in a small restaurant eating a sandwich when the counterman sidled up. "Want my sister? She very clean."

Uncommon Value

Many hotels have a system of security guards to keep the whores in the lobby and prevent them from wandering the halls above. In keeping with all this there is a very rich erotic art. Some old, much recent. Some subtle and delicate, some ribald and crude. There is a good market for the better older erotic art, especially in Germany.

In the days when the United States was a major economic force, we had an airline that circled the globe. Pan Am, Juan Trippe's airline was the only American carrier that had flights around the world. We no longer have a global airline. Pan Am flight 1 used to go in one direction, Flight 2 in the other. I forget which was which, but I used to take Pan Am on my extended business trips. Only once did I go eastward, and the jet lag was so uncomfortable that I never did it again. I would usually cross the Pacific to Japan, then travel to Hong Kong and on to Thailand. From there I would take the Pan Am flight continuing to Delhi.

The Pan Am flight to Delhi always arrived in the very early morning, shortly after midnight. Apparently there was some problem that prevented Pan Am from getting a landing slot at a decent time. Other carriers didn't seem to have this difficulty. I recall the first time I landed in Delhi. We climbed down the airplane ladder and walked across the gravel to the terminal. The terminal reminded me, from the outside, as a nothing than an unusually big 'operations shack' that we itinerant pilots were used to in the United States. Glaring overhead lights attracted huge bugs. Beetles the size of hamsters scurried underfoot. Step on one of those babies, and splat! there goes a pair of shoes. Massed humanity filled the terminal. There was no place to go that wasn't crammed with people. All this at three AM. A time when airports elsewhere in the world are empty.

My first taxi ride from the airport to my hotel, the Akbar, was uneventful. I wasn't as fortunate a couple of years later. I guess the political and economic climate had worsened a bit. Again I arrived via Pan Am at some ungodly hour. Tired, hungry, dirty. I took a taxi to Delhi, this time I was staying at the Imperial on the Janpath. I began to doze off as the taxi left the airport; the driver had a companion, his 'mechanic' in the left seat. We drove a while into an increasing rural area. The driver stopped for petrol, for which he hadn't any money. I paid the petrol bill for him and noticed that both he and his 'mechanic' looked into my wallet as I paid. I had a wad of bills. Back in the taxi. I in the rear and the two Indians in the front. The road got more and more rugged; no lights, no pavement. Clearly we were not on the road to Delhi. When the jungle began to encroach on the road, I became alarmed. When I travel in places like this, I always carry a knife in my pocket. Unfortunately I had just gotten off an airplane and the knife had been checked with my baggage which was now stowed in the taxi's boot. What to do? I tried to fill the back of the taxi with my mass as much as possible, I leaned over the seat into the drivers compartment and slammed my fist into my hand.

"Take me to Delhi. Now!" I snarled directions to them in my deepest voice. They turned around and I hunched my shoulders, trying to look as well as sound large and mean. I hadn't the foggiest idea where we were, certainly we were nowhere near a major road and we had not been going in the direction of Delhi. I was terrified and quite prepared to cause some major damage to the heads in front of me, and I think they knew it. They turned the taxi around and finally drove me into town. Heart rate up, adrenalin up and anger and fear at equal levels, I continued to look angry and mean. Still, they couldn't quite bring themselves to do as told. Instead of taking me to the Imperial, they stopped at some fleabag in a back alley and wouldn't go on. By now morning was here and light was welcomed back. There was another taxi in sight, a welcome one, certainly! I paid the two goons what I thought I owed them and despite the expectation of the masses of children crowding around the hotel to which I'd been brought, I jumped into the other taxi and fled to the Imperial.

Uncommon Value

I later learned that there had been several murders. Foreigners coming in from the airport late at night had disappeared. To try to control this, the government had set up a military checkpoint at the airport and every taxi leaving with a passenger was supposed to register. I recall that we had stopped at a little kiosk, but nobody was there. I was free game for them. I'm quite convinced that they would have killed me for the money they knew was in my wallet. Shades of Chicago! This was the closest I'd come to getting killed outside the US.

Each time I went to Delhi I visited several dealers, most of whom had foreign offices with which I had traded. It was important to see them here and meet with them personally on their owe turf. Our visits were always pleasant. I would also go and visit another wonderful dealer. He was an exceptionally sensitive individual who was trying to become known as a filmmaker. His only child, a daughter, was one of the most treasured kids I've ever known. Paul acted as an intermediary for me. I bought hundreds of little paintings from him. These were a form of Indian cottage industry at the time. Artists, some more skilled than others, copied scenes from old Mughal works. These weren't just copies, rather, they were copied onto old book pages so that they looked like ancient miniatures. The artists would buy old manuscript books, usually school copybooks such as grammar exercises, and using opaque pigments, would copy a classical scene onto old book leaves. Hey Presto! they looked real and seemed at first glance to be original old miniatures torn from books. Most were sold to westerners who could not read the manuscript text. These were very attractive decorative little paintings and I had a ready market for them in the US.

This form of overpainting is known as a palimpsest. The technique is an old one, the artist simply applies an opaque coat to mask the underlying image and then applies a new one. Palimpsests are hard to detect if done well, even a very strong light transilluminating the page often will fail to reveal an image under the one visible. This is quite common in oil painting, where the pigments are opaque. Older paintings sometimes have another, hidden, image underneath. Such images can often be revealed by X-ray analysis.

The Indian paper palimpsests can sometimes be tricky to detect. Many elegant little shops in hotel arcades sold these miniatures to tourists and would palm them off as antique paintings. Typically the proprietor would keep a few in a carved wooden box and when someone inquired about them, he would take them out, one at time, with all the ostentatious care befitting each precious leaf. The page would then be lain on a black velvet cloth and illuminated with a good (but not too good) light. It was always a very impressive presentation but I have never seen a truly original leaf in any of these shops. Tourists would naturally assume that the paintings were authentic since the leaves themselves were obviously old.

Most of the time the poorer paintings are obvious on stylistic grounds alone. Of course, if one could read the text they would all be very easy to detect. The text and the picture bear no relation to each other. Scenes from a Sha-na-ma on a page of grammar clearly cannot be correct. I've even seen some where the painting was placed on an upside down text. There's another trick that's helpful in detecting these fakes. Many of the manuscript pages the artists used were heavily wormed. When the artist painted the image, the paint ran through the little wormholes and formed a colored ring on the other side. If the historical sequence were correct, the worms would have eaten through the completed page, painting and all, and there would be no paint leaked through their holes. It's surprising how just a little thought about a process will permit us to detect many fakes. These were beautiful little leaves and they sold well. I imported hundreds each year, selling them inexpensively as attractive little paintings with no claim to antiquity. However they were perhaps too beautiful and were being sold as original antique Mughal paintings by some of the dealers who bought them from me. The market is still filled with spurious leaves and most people cannot tell that they are inexpensive modern paintings, the product of a little Indian cottage industry.

I didn't relish anymore nighttime taxi rides to Delhi and changed airlines so that I arrived in Delhi during broad daylight. This had another benefit. I could look out the plane windows and see the fascinating countryside below. So incredibly ancient with thousands of years of human habitation and human alterations to the landscape. Buried beneath almost every field must be layer upon layer of old foundations, villages and cities. From the air their ghosts are visible, creating spectral alterations to the vegetation above.

And the Himalayas. The first time I saw them from the starboard side of the airplane I could not quite believe they were mountains. Their sheer mass on a global scale was overwhelming. Comparisons will not do. No simile is adequate to convey the humanness that is felt from the juxtaposition of one's self to these mountains, even at the great distance that separated those of us in the airplane from the hills. A daylight flight into India is clearly the choice.

Chapter 10

Istanbul

I have approached Istanbul from both Europe and Asia. This remarkable city presents different flavors to visitors arriving from different directions. It can display either chunks or hints of virtually any culture, European and Asian, behind the blend that is its very soul. The complexities of every aspect of this city are so vast that probably every impression possible has some validity. We can find whatever we need to see, the city is like some magic mirror, reflecting back to us part of its inner self. But the mirror is not flat, and introduces puzzling, perplexing distortions that become part of the reality of the place.

Istanbul is a sensuous city, filled with smells, textures and sights that will never leave me. I recall, still with wonder, the first time I heard sound of the muezzin calling the faithful to prayers, his scratchy voice carried on a miserable sound system that blared from atop a minaret. I remember the smell of kerosene heaters filling the November air and rising up to my balcony in the old Park Oteli. Alas, the old Park Oteli is no more. Once a splendid hotel, built along the side of a steep hill overlooking the Bosphorus, it was torn down some years ago, I think in the early '70's. Coming off Taksim Square, one entered the lobby and descended to the rooms below. Heavy old carpets, dark mahogany panels, everything so very European as only true Turkish style enables.

Istanbul, as every major city, changes. But in its own way, at its own terms. Hip, modern, fast-paced and international, nonetheless there are people here who live a thousand years ago. The steep cobbled streets wind around and only recently do the donkey carts and the stooped hamals, those human donkeys with huge loads on their permanently bent backs fade from the scene. Streets are now congested with Mercedes, some chauffeured, some filled with poor workers. Busses trucks vans cars people all in a state of seeming chaos. Hip and old. The city is so very old. I crossed the same threshold that Justinian crossed. I stood where the walls were breached in the 15th Century and the city fell to cannon firing Turks. Ancient aqueducts, ancient markets, domed mosques, and all populated by the most hospitable big city people anywhere. Except when they're blowing up trolley cars during some period of political unrest. Even then, even when the Red Brigades were at their worst and the government was reacting with force, I always felt that Turkey, and especially Istanbul were very special.

In the early eighties I had visited the old Soviet Union to spend a couple of weeks hunting wild boar in Azerbaijan. Leaving that splendid old city on the Caspian Sea, Baku, that once belonged to Turkey, I went deep into the Caucasus on the hunt. A hunting trip that I will never forget. Great companions, great food and great scenery. The Azerbaijanis were the best hosts and hunting companions I have ever had.

I had planned to go to Istanbul after the hunt and ship my gear back home. Since I was going on eastward to Japan where I had some business that needed attention, I didn't want to lug my hunting gear across all of Asia. But in order to get to Turkey I had to first fly from Baku to Moscow and then back to Ankara. I could have walked from Baku.

Soviet officials barked. I was sick of it and wanted out. Communists were surly downtroddens. Civility had left them along with the Romanoffs. I was the only person on the little bus that took passengers from the VIP terminal at Sheremetyevo to the waiting plane. My penultimate experience with Soviet officialdom was the uniformed official in the bus with me. He got up, stood towering in front of me and barked. Instead of 'bow-wow' he barked "Passport!" In as rude and intimidating manner as possible he snatched it from my hand, tore out the removable visa and thrust it back.

"Thank you, Generalissimo."

After takeoff, the Aeroflot stewardess barked at us few passengers that we were not to take any pictures from the airplane and gave us each a cup of water, probably laced heavily with parasitic Giardia. As soon as we were in Turkish airspace, I took my Leica from its case and ostentatiously photographed the free land below. When I got off the Aeroflot in Ankara to change planes I saw several Turkish soldiers guarding the airport against hijackers. Bristling with Uzzis and seemingly every other possible weapon, they looked ominous. But they were laughing and joking and I knew I was back in freedom. Spontaneous laughter marks the boundary between totalitarianism and freedom better than barbed wire or electric fences. That night I slept soundly, back at the Pera Palas, back home in free Istanbul.

The Pera Palas, opened in 1894 and built by La Compagnie Internationale des Wagons-Lits (of Orient Express fame) is the dowager queen of Istanbul hotels. Located in the old embassy area on the heights of Pera, the Hotel still flaunts the icons of the Belle Epoque. The birdcage elevator with the broad sweeping staircase built around it, the crystal chandeliers in the great ballroom and thick, faded velvet drapes. Eclipsed by the giants of the hotel industry, the Pera Palas continues on. Having hosted Agatha Christie, Edward VIII, Sarah Bernhardt, F.J. Manasek and Greta Garbo; served as local color for Graham Greene and Eric Ambler, the hotel is now an official Turkish landmark.

Uncommon Value

I like to think I had a bit of a role in this. Whenever I arrived there, the bartenders were inept at making good martinis.

"Chin martini? Evet." Ha!

However, after a few days of my patient tutelage they invariably became masters of the art. Equally invariate was their subsequent departure to either the Hilton or Intercontinental. I then had to start over with a fresh one the next time. I think it is clear that Turkish officials got wind that somehow, the Pera Palas converted simple barkeeps, rustics from the wilds of Anatolia into the *ustas* of the martini. Clearly a national treasure needing to be preserved.

Elizabeth could always be dislodged from her Aegean hideaway to spend time with me in Istanbul. She had, in the late 70's fled England, leaving behind both London and her tweed and riding boot weekends, for the quiet and peace of the Greek islands. Elizabeth, a painter of some note, loved the people, the islands and the light and captured all three with her brushes. Despite her self imposed exile, Elizabeth needed the occasional "city fix" and our times together in Istanbul provided that. We walked the old city together until it seemed we had been there all our lives. I treasure still the little pleasures of marketing for our splendid picnic lunches overlooking the Bosphorus north of the city; her happiness and soft smile over long dinners. Her quiet laughter is borne still by the soft wind that flows down the Bosphorus; she is part of that permanent memory of the City. I think the weeks, days and hours we spent together are the finest yet caressed by the timelessness of that ancient place.

Turkey, a country filled with classical treasure, has seen much of it looted and hauled away. The Turks now have a strong set of antiquities acts, laws that prohibit the exportation of antiquities. This has effectively closed the legal antiques trade to the outside. It is true that many items are still smuggled out of the country but the immorality of this is evident if we consider for but a moment how we would feel if the contents of our Colonial Williamsburg were being smuggled out. And the consequences of breaking Turkish law. Watch the movie *Midnight Express* if you want to learn about deterrence. Nonetheless, the temptation to smuggle out antiquities is very great, the profits seem to be enormous and the crime is considered more white collar than smuggling hash. Years ago I was at the bar in the Pera Palas, helping the bartender upgrade his skills. A lanky American sat down next to me and began talking. I soon realized that he was lonely and was trying to hit on me. I was lonely also, but only to hear native English. I hadn't spoken English for a month or so and it was nice to hear an American accent again. Tom had been drinking heavily and was more than a bit indiscreet. He was an antiquities smuggler. He apparently took things to his contact in Germany, a gay member of German nobility. The German, in return for favors, would provide a fake provenance for the smuggled items, attesting that they had been in his family's possession for a hundred years, or whatever. Tom was very pleased with himself. He had recently sold some very fine oriental antiquities to a famous institute in Chicago. According to him, the director knew that the provenance was fake, but the buy was too good to turn down. Besides, every American loves a nobleman, which is why the cover was so good. I never found out if this was true or if Tom was a plant by the Turkish secret police trying to catch smugglers. I got away from him as soon as possible and never found out who Tom was and never tried to find out if any institute in Chicago had bought any Turkish antiquities from a noble German family. If they had, I suppose they wouldn't have been the first things that they acquired via the back door.

Islam and the printing press did not get along. The Turks did not have a press until a few hundred years ago and as a consequence there are no native printed images of old Turkey, as there are of England, any European country or city and even America. All of the early printed images of Turkey and Istanbul, or Constantinople, are foreign. The Turks have an almost insatiable appetite for these, including the books in which they are found. In particular, there is a

Uncommon Value

steady market for Julia Pardoe's *Beauties of the Bosphorus,* a wonderful 19th Century work heavily illustrated with Bartlett's steelplate engravings. For years I had a great trade selling this book, and other similar ones, into the Turkish market. Good copies found their way into the libraries of the affluent Istanbulis; damaged copies were taken apart for the illustrations. Sold in many antique shops in the city and in all the better hotel arcades, these prints capture the sights of a city no longer. So popular are they that reproductions, excessively enlarged, have been published. Colored garishly they decorate many hotel rooms.

The covered bazaar is one of the great experiences of the city. One can wander for days through its labyrinthian reaches. Segregated by trades, there are parts of the bazaar that specialize in carpets, copperware, clothing, leather and a myriad of others. Some supply the essential goods and services that any city and its occupants needs.

Vast sections are devoted to jewelry and the glimmer of gold in the brightly lighted shops, accentuated by the gloom and general poor light of the corridors makes a wonderful sight. In the past, the women wore their fortunes on their arms in the form of gold bracelets. With only a minimum of decorative work, gold was fashioned into simple arm hoops and sold for just a bit over melt value. It was indeed a form of currency and one still sees Turkish women displaying vast numbers of such gold bracelets.

Others cater to the tourist and visitor. These are the places where a shopkeeper can speak enough of five or six languages to consummate any deal. I never found anything of age or particular value in the antiques or curio section of the bazaar, although it was one of the most interesting areas. Once, I casually picked up a large, coarse halftone color lithograph, probably from a calendar, of a Turkish miniature painting. It was in a cheap frame behind dusty glass.

"Original, original!" cried the shopkeeper.

F.J. Manasek

Near the top of the Tunel, the funicular that carries one up and down the steep hill at Galata, is a small square that houses several newspaper and magazine dealers, a couple of airline offices and the small shop of the Cohen sisters. The sisters Cohen, many years ago, fled one of the many pogroms that afflicted Jews living in Russia. As did many of the refugees, the Cohens fled southward and got to Istanbul. The Turks, contrary to what many in the West believe, have a long tradition of tolerance. After the Spanish *reconquista,* the Jews who were forced to flee were welcomed by the Sultan. The Jews who fled both the old Czars and the new, the communists, found refuge here as well. Istanbul is a city filled with foreigners, and even though they don't like to admit it, there is a prosperous Greek community here. For thousands of years this town has absorbed outsiders.

It was into this cosmopolitan city, a haven to waves of immigrants, that the Cohen sisters fled with their old books. Nobody knows just how many books they took with them, but for years there seemed to be an inexhaustible supply of them. It seems amazing to me that people fleeing for their lives should take with them books to be used as commodities in their new land. The currency of choice was of course gold or diamonds — something more readily portable than trunks of books. Nonetheless, books is what it was and the Cohen sisters made a reasonably good living selling new magazines and newspapers and their old books. They were nearing the end of their inventory when I first met them. I cannot guess their ages, they appeared to be old, as in very old. Repeated visits to the shop began to result in the appearance of a few books now and then. Bertha and I got along, although we had extreme difficulty communicating. She was fluent in Turkish, Russian, French and Yiddish. I suspect she spoke German but just refused to do so on principle. My languages were English, Spanish, German and at that time, some Japanese. My French was pitiable and I had but a hundred words of Turkish. I could use this Turkish vocabulary to travel, count, buy food and find the toilet but not talk with Bertha Cohen. Nonetheless we managed, although how well,

Uncommon Value

I'll never know. Through one of our many linguistic encounters, she decided that I had a wife in Israel. When I tried to explain that I didn't, and that indeed, I wasn't even married, Bertha understood. She patted my arm and gave me the most wonderful conspiratorial looks I've ever received. "It's all right. I understand," she conveyed knowingly. Whatever the hell she understood, I'll never know. After establishing that my wife was in Israel, Bertha Cohen sold me some nice books. Never very many at a time, they were always metered out to me. I looked forward to my visits with the Cohens, and despite the difficulty of communicating we always got along and I like to think that they enjoyed seeing me. I was sorry when they died and their little shop disappeared from the face of Istanbul. I walk by there once in a while and think of the sisters Cohen and the city that outlives us all.

The city is built straddling two continents separated by the Bosphorus. There is a wing of water, the Golden Horn, that separates old Stamboul from the newer reaches of Pera and Galata to the north. This blind inlet, once a clean, pure stretch of water has become foul and polluted, partly as a result of the Galata Bridge which interrupted the cleansing ebb and flow of the waters from the Marmara. Somewhere along the reaches of this inlet, in one of the poorer sections of the city, is a mosque where I went to worship when I was in town. One of the book dealers in the courtyard of the Beyazit mosque, the Beyazit Çarshi, was an immam. Mustafa Ozak had a little corner shop in the sun drenched square. There was a small garden and a fountain in the middle of the square and the shops built into the wall housed a curious assortment of used bookshops. Most of them sold second hand copies of modern Turkish works, and their trade was brisk. There were always browsers and buyers standing at the outside displays. In size and character, these shops reminded me of the little freestanding bookshops in Madrid, where lots of old books, none very valuable, are traded.

F.J. Manasek

Mustafa Ozak was Immam of a Dervish sect. Once outlawed, Dervishes still keep a low profile in the secular state of Turkey. I always brought some things to sell to Mustafa Ozak and our relationship was a very pleasant one. I accepted his invitation to worship with his congregation and was picked up at my hotel by a group of young people. We drove into the Istanbul night, shunning the major arteries. At once, I became lost. I know only that we drove along the Golden Horn for a distance and then plunged again into a maze of alleys and sidestreets. We left the car and continued on foot, briskly walking through back yards, alleys, past barking dogs and yowling cats. The mosque itself, no Sinan influence here, was a simple structure attached to adjacent buildings. Inside, I had a simple meal in the presence of the Immam and then went in to pray. Women were segregated in an anteroom, spectral outlines only behind a thick mesh. The service was a long, pulsating, sensuous, throbbing experience, with scores of men, each having his own experience, but in unison with the body congregation.

Mustafa Ozak has since died and I no longer go to worship. I no longer bring books to Istanbul and carry away in turn those wonderful memories worth more than all the armlets in the gold bazaar. My trips to Istanbul now are antiseptic events to call upon the tiny handful of map dealers who have developed a trade among the growing middle class. More often, we meet in Europe and conduct our business in Frankfurt or Berlin or Munich. Maps. Marks. Dollars. Handshake. 747 home. I make a lot more money doing it this way but I will never get treasures more from Istanbul than Elizabeth's laughter and the wonderful book given to me by Mustafa Ozak. Inscribed.

Chapter 11

Auctions

Reality sets in quickly after returning home from time abroad. Business must be attended to and, hopefully, inventory replenished on the shelves. Perhaps no other method of buying and selling inventory is more misunderstood than the auction. In the old days, book auctions served to disseminate goods to the trade and were patronized largely by dealers. Some years ago, led by the major name-brand auction houses, there was a concerted advertising effort to convince the collecting public that auctions were the ideal place to buy privately. The auction houses changed their images dramatically in an effort to become 'buyer friendly.' Modest printed catalogues became large, illustrated glossy publications and included printed estimates of the prices the house expected the items would fetch. When dealers were the principal buyers at auction there was little need for the house to provide price guidelines. I recall feeling a bit of dismay when even Swann Galleries in New York began to put estimated price ranges in their catalogues. I knew what things should go for, if others did not, that was their problem. I think it is a two edged sword. Many amateurs tend to pay too much at auction and house estimates have often kept this tendency checked, reducing the amount the consignors received.

F.J. Manasek

Auction houses, especially the famous English firms, really developed airs and began to try to pass themselves off as institutions rather than businesses. Private buyers flocked to the auctions which became social events as well as markets. An essentially whole new industry was created that competed head on with the traditional role of the dealer. Thus there developed a growing competition and animosity between dealers and auction houses.

One of the reasons why this happened is perhaps that the nature of collecting, at least in books and maps, began to change. New collectors were flocking in, their interest primed in part by the seeming attractive rates of appreciation that books, maps, and especially art, offered. This was particularly true in the late 70's and early 80's when inflation in this country was double digit and money was flowing into durable goods. Collectors were a 'modern generation' more used to making their own decisions and they had the leisure time to go and chase their own quarry. Perhaps they found the traditional dealers too stuffy. Certainly, it became quite trendy to buy at Sotheby's.

New York's venerable auction house at the time was the Park Bernet Galleries. You still can tell a veteran. They pronounce Bernet correctly, sounding the final "t". Newcomers almost invariably say "Bernay." Sotheby's invaded and took over the Park Bernet Galleries. With the infusion of additional capitol, SPB expanded rapidly and soon had several locations in New York; different price level goods were sold in different locations.

Do I buy at auctions? Of course I do, as do all of my colleagues. However, I can no longer buy general inventory at most sales. The competition from private collectors is too great and much of the general stock I used to buy at auction now fetches far more than I could get for it in my own business. There are a number of reasons for this. I think that clever marketing by the big houses was responsible for the idea that one could buy 'at wholesale' because this is 'where the dealers buy.' Every dealer I know has stories of clients

Uncommon Value

who turned down an offered item, only to buy a similar or even lesser one at auction for far more money. These same people are also convinced that dealers charge too much and that they have beaten the system somehow, by circumventing the dealer and buying directly at auction. I take advantage of this phenomenon and consign unsold inventory to the auction houses where it generally fetches more than I would have gotten for it in a direct sale. This phenomenon was not discovered by me. Local New England auctions attract a lot of tourists and city folk, especially in the summer. One of the better known local auctioneers regularly gets consignments of unsold furniture from New York City antiques dealers. More often than not, they get higher prices than they would in New York.

There are certainly some items that need to be presented to a global audience and sold with the forces of a global market in place. I think of major paintings as such items. But I don't think that good maps and books generally selling in the low thousands need, or even profit from being sold this way. For one thing, auction house commissions are not trivial, and the less expensive the item the greater is the proportion of the commission paid to the house. Then come the miscellaneous charges, the insurance, the cataloging fee, the illustration fee, the storage fee and if it doesn't sell, the minimum reserve fee. By the time a consignor is done with these fees, the check he gets some six months or a year later is a good deal reduced. A very reputable London dealer is running a very informative ad. He is trying to let potential sellers know that all is not skittles and beer when dealing with auction houses. His ad reads "The best auctioneers now take 20% of the final price: the worst take over 30%" To which I add, "If you're lucky."

On the other side of the hammer, auction buyers now are faced with a 15% surcharge, called a buyer's premium. This has no function other than to increase the auction house's profit. In England this buyer's premium is subject to the VAT, or an additional 17%. VAT on buyer's premiums is not refundable even if the item is taken out of the country. The true cost of buying at auction is really a lot higher than the advertised hammer price. Of course, dealers know that most commissions and fees are negotiable and that there is no reason to accept the house terms. After all, we are hiring them! Major buyers know to discuss their charges as well.

One of the most pernicious problems of buying at auctions involves condition and guarantees. If you buy from a dealer's catalogue and the item is not what you thought it was, or even if you just decided you didn't want it, you can return it. That might not make the dealer very happy and if you did it a lot you might not remain a client, but nonetheless an item you had just bought should be returnable. Try that with an auction house! If you buy something it's yours. In most cases there are no warranties. In many cases, if you buy a stolen item at auction, you're out of luck. Strange as it may seem, if you unknowingly buy hot items at an auction and the owner recovers his goods, you have no recourse except to try to recover from the consignor. The auction house is not liable. This is not just theoretical speculation. I know of one case at the present time where an American collector bought an atlas at a major London auction house. He received a letter recently from the auction house informing him that the atlas had been stolen. The owner wants it back and the house has no liability.

The possibility for auction flimflam is quite large, much larger than in a regular dealer's trade. Take for example absentee bidding. One needn't be present at an auction. One can leave a bid with the house, this bid should be executed on your behalf as though you wherein the audience bidding openly. In most cases this is what happens. However, the temptation to jack up the bids is very real. Suppose you leave a bid of a thousand dollars on a lot. Bidding on the floor stops at five hundred. The house should bid on your behalf at the next increment, say $550. If there are no other bids from the floor, that would be it. The item would be yours for $550., plus of course the 15% buyers premium and

Uncommon Value

the VAT. However, the house could easily invent another absentee bid, say at $800. You would then 'buy' the item at the next increment, or $850. plus 15% buyers premium plus VAT. The advantage to the house is the increased commission from the consignor and the additional buyer's premium. Even if one attends an auction in person there is no guarantee that this won't happen and we often find ourselves bidding against the chandelier.

The concept of a 'reserve' is interesting. A reserve is the minimum price for which a lot may be sold. This figure is supposed to be kept secret from the bidders and known only to the house and consignor. Most houses have minimum bids and these in effect are reserves. Thus, if there is no interest in a thousand dollar item, you are not going to get it for fifty bucks. The house is likely to have a reserve of at least 50% of the lower estimate. Most often the reserve is higher, having been agreed upon between house and consignor. In New York State, the reserve cannot be greater than the top estimate, in other places there are no such laws.

So far it sounds good. The reserve protects the consignor against taking a major bath. However, if the reserve is too high then the item won't sell. The consignor gets it back but still owes the house a commission. If it sells you pay, if it doesn't you pay. Since the reserve can be fixed by agreement between the house and consignor and since it is a secret number, it can be changed without anyone knowing it. Herein lies one of the more ingenious ripoffs. Let us assume that someone consigns a thousand dollar item and agrees to a five hundred dollar reserve. The consignor later learns, possibly from the auction house itself, that there is one absentee bid for $2000. The lot should open at $500. (the reserve) and go up one increment to $550., with the house bidding for the absentee bidder who left a $2000. bid. If there is no bidding from the floor that's it; the lot has gone above reserve for $550. to the chap who was willing to pay $2000. The consignor, being no fool, raises his reserve to

F.J. Manasek

$1900. Now the lot opens at $1900.and is knocked down to the absentee bidder who bid $2000.

Playing games with reserves is even more tempting in the circumstances when the house may own outright, or have a financial interest in, items they are auctioning. In those circumstances any way the house can jump a bid is a potential way to increase profits enormously, and since it owns the lots it can set any reserve it wants at any time it wants. Even five minutes before the sale begins when all the absentee bids are in. I have made it a rule never to bid when there is such a conflict of interest. Some auction houses will indicate when they own part of or all of a lot that is appearing in one of their sales. Others do not. I am especially leery about the smaller private auctions scattered around the country. Some of these are owned by, or affiliated with, book dealers, and may represent nothing more than a merchandising scheme for selling books. The fact that some of these will accept consignments doesn't alter the picture. I do not ever buy or sell at a book auction that is affiliated with a private book dealer. The conflict of interest is too great.

New Hampshire has just had another auction scandal. Seems that owners of property that was being auctioned were bidding on their own behalf to drive up the prices. This was going on with the knowledge of the auctioneer. The case made all the local and trade papers and there may be prosecutions resulting. None of that would help you if you were stung and found you had to get involved in a New Hampshire lawsuit to extricate yourself.

There may never be any way to prevent an auctioneer from calling on fake bids from the floor to drive up the price, nor to prevent shills from doing some fake bidding, but we should at least be aware of the practice. I was told a story a few years ago that if not true, at least should be. A map and atlas sale at a major London house was going along quite briskly with record prices being fetched. A well known, perhaps notorious, American dealer was thick in the bidding wars. Finally, sensing that something was not quite right with the way the bids were going, he watched the floor more carefully. He is credited with finally calling out in a loud voice, disrupting the sale, "Hey, you SOB, you're picking fake bids off the wall!"

Years ago consignors of goods to auctions were getting ripped off by the ring. The ring represented a group of dealers who agreed not to bid against each other at the sale. They would then acquire the choice lots at artificially low prices and after the sale was over would meet privately where they apportioned the lots in their own auction, or the 'knockdown' Rings were particularly prevalent in England where the practice became so widespread that it became illegal. Indeed, taking part in a ring will result in expulsion from the major trade association, the Antiquarian Booksellers' Association. Rings still exist, but they generally are less organized and more informal. In general, they are quiet agreement between two or three individuals not to bid against each other on certain lots. Technically this is illegal. In the large salesrooms in London rings would have a hard time since a few dealers do not control the prices, but in smaller provincial salesrooms, rings still operate.

In the past few years there have been two notable failures of auction houses. In one case, a book auction on the West Coast had been experiencing financial difficulties for a few years and despite continued input of money from the owner was not going to make it. They had scheduled their annual rare book sale and successfully solicited consignments for it. The sale went well, and after most of the receipts had been collected but before the consignors received their money they declared bankruptcy. It might have been a coincidence, but I don't think so. A similar thing happened involving a well known East Coast auction house that dealt primarily in antiques. I'm not quite certain if one can protect oneself from this kind of auction house danger.

Auctioneers are not dealers. They do not (and should not) have their own money tied up in inventory. They are more like open pit mines. They create a mechanism for processing huge amounts of product. As in mining, their raw material, the consignment, is non-renewable. The auction market is such that if an item reappears on the block before a few years have intervened since its last appearance, it will likely flop. This audience, with much in common with the Roman circus audience is fickle and has come to demand 'fresh' material. Sooner or later, the mine runs out and there is no more new 'fresh' material coming on the market. This day can be put off, although not forever, by constantly raising the ante and both promising and delivering ever increasing prices for things. Of course, along with record prices come the press releases and more buying demand.

The ever increasing demand for material places the auction house and the private dealer in competition. Auctions have always had a bit of glamor associated with them, they have even more now with the new publicity and the new direction of the major houses. I think they are winning the battle for goods; fewer people sell them to dealers, preferring to place them at auction. Not content with this, auctions are trying to take away retail business as well from the dealers. I used to have a client who bought astronomical atlases. Whenever I had a particularly nice one I would offer it to him. I once had a pristine copy of the Doppelmaier atlas, published about 1740. It was beautiful, with original color, snowy white pages, sound original binding and untrimmed edges. It was not cheap. I think a lesser or average Doppelmaier would have fetched, in those days, about $4000. Mine was $6000. and that was without apology for the price. It was that beautiful. My client bought it and was very happy with the condition. A few weeks later, he happened to be talking with the book department of one of the big London auction houses. One of their 'experts' told him he had grossly overpaid and that I had cheated him. Of course, he should return this atlas to me and wait until one came up at Christoby's where it would be much, if not much much cheaper. After all this is where dealers buy and auction prices are fair, as we all know. Rob believed him and returned the atlas to me, firmly believing that I had overcharged him. I don't know if he ever got his bargain Doppelmaier from Sotheby's, but I do know that if he did, it was in lesser condition. I also hope that Rob has, in the meantime, tried to return to Christoby's, for a cheery refund, something he bought a month earlier. I also note that the last current price on the same atlas in lesser condition than mine was eleven thousand dollars.

The big auction houses can manipulate prices in many ways. If they fear the market is about to fall, they can pump money into a sale by lending money to individuals who then use the loan to buy, say a painting, and set a new record price. The newly valued painting is then used as collateral for the original loan. After all, the price was established at auction and we all know that auction prices determine the value of an item. This sort of thing works until the day comes when the prices no longer go up and someone is left holding the bag. It will be the last bidder to have raised his paddle, and not the house.

Not all is dark and sinister with auction houses. They have always provided a service to consignor, collector and dealer and still do. They just need to be viewed in the proper perspective.

Chapter 12

Fairs

███████████████████████

    It is difficult in this world, which is not knee-deep in buyers of rare books or maps, for us dealers to meet clients. It is equally difficult for collectors and potential collectors to discover, examine and buy rare items. Things might be a little easier if both dealer and collector lived and worked in London, New York or Vienna, but, alas, such is not the case for most of us. Ordinary used bookshops can thrive on a completely local trade. They will buy and sell within the local community, their trade will reflect the reading and buying habits of that community. A shop such as this, when it by chance or luck gets a book or map that the proprietor is uncomfortable with selling, or cannot because he doesn't have the customers or knowledge to do so, sells it to another dealer. Often it doesn't ever appear on the shelves.

    As soon as one begins to deal in more esoteric items, marketing becomes very different and sometimes difficult. It doesn't matter where one's shop or office is, but if one has in stock 16th century world maps, Thai divination manuscripts, medieval manuscripts, Islamic manuscripts, 18th century physics and astronomy and a robust selection of 17th and 18th century maps by major mapmakers, then there is no location in the world past which buyers will flow. This selection represents my inventory and although somewhat

Uncommon Value

more diverse than that of other dealers, the problem is the same. We have to somehow contact collectors in our subject areas.

Advertising doesn't work very well. There are too few collectors spread too thin to reach them by conventional advertising means. I used to run occasional ads in the New York Times and in various antiques magazines. They usually brought lunatic-fringe responses, but precious few serious enquiries. I remember getting poorly penned letters such as "Dear Sirs. Please send me all the free antique maps of Poland." Other letters would go into lengthy, circuitous details about some old town or city and ask me to send Xerox copies of maps that show these regions. I was offered all sorts of maps to buy and would get the occasional package of "rare maps" for which the sender would want outrageous sums and which, out of sheer kindness, I would send back.

The few map collector publications that exist are splendid magazines but do not reach new audiences. Only diehard collectors subscribe to them; they all know me and I know all of them. No new business here. Book collecting is similarly problemed. "Book collector" is too broad a category. Most collectors do not collect in broad categories, but collect in very specific areas. As a specialist dealer, the trick is to contact these specialist collectors both in maps and books.

Since I, and virtually all other specialist dealers, both map and book, depend upon mail order business we must have some way of meeting the specialist collectors and establishing a business relationship with them. The fair is such a medium.

Fairs are ancient events. We have records of medieval fairs and know that from time immemorial merchants have gathered to display wares and goods and customers have attended to root through the displays and compare and, hopefully, buy. It matters not whether one is at a livestock, garden produce, home furnishing or antique map fair, the basic pattern is the same: a merchant rents space and displays the wares and the public come and view.

In my earlier days in this business I was dealing extensively in Japanese art, mostly woodblock prints and scrolls. My venue was the antique fair. I soon learned that not all antique fairs are equal. Although I developed a nice following at the better fairs held in major cities, I bombed in the hinterland. Perhaps the most notable of these bombs was a fair I did in the late 1970's, in Indianapolis, Indiana. Other dealers had recommended this fair highly. The organizer was experienced and the fair was alleged to be one of the best. I gave it a try, and drove to the Indiana Fairgrounds where the antiques fair was held. Setup was uneventful but the usual crush of other dealers that come visit as one is setting up in order to get first dibs on the goods was missing. I had a large aluminum frame on which I hung a dozen or so fine Japanese scrolls and had stacks of woodblock prints on tables. I hung a few Hiroshige prints which I knew were going to attract the buyers. A few booths down from me, Les Werbel of the Lotus Gallery in Ann Arbor was setting up also. He had splendid oriental artifacts, some prints, especially a wonderful group of Hsui shin-hanga prints. He and I were confident; this was going to be a great fair.

When we were set up and had time to look around we began to have first doubts. The entire fair was filled with dealers in depression glass, country furniture and 'smalls.' Smalls are just that — little things. Candlesticks, corkscrews, fly swatters, ash trays, book ends, vases, nail clippers. Some were quite good but there was a lot of repro stuff around also. I had one sale the entire fair. Les Werbel bought a print from me. Fair visitors would wander into my booth, look at the prints briefly and begin to laugh. They thought the images funny. When they took the time to look at the price tags, they found it even funnier.

Les had the same experience, except that I think he sold two items. In addition to the print I bought from him,

Uncommon Value

someone else bought something. It was a good lesson in selecting venues.

One small provincial antiques fair at which I used to exhibit was held on the campus of Notre Dame, in South Bend. It was a nice show, small and reasonably select. Held in the athletic arena, the second most important site on the Notre Dame campus, it drew widely from the academic community as well as the more affluent parts of South Bend. Even so, it was fraught with curious happenings. I had a nice display of vellum manuscript leaves from bibles and books of hours dating from about 1300 to about 1500. An elegant young South Bend matron looked at the display, noted the descriptive cards, looked at me and in as haughty a voice as a true Hoosier could muster asked "Where would you get something like this?"

Notre Dame, although it has a loyal following, is perhaps not one of the great intellectual centers. Many professors had an ecclesiastical view of information. If word came from them it had to be true by virtue of their rank. One of the people from the art history department used to bring students over to my booth and expound on the Japanese prints. I once made the mistake of correcting him and was told in no uncertain terms that he was a Professor and I was a dealer and I should know my place. Fortunately I do know my place, just as he knew his and I bet South Bend, Indiana is still "where he's at." *Hier bin Ich; wo bist Du?*

Antiques fairs were not the best venue for selling paper. People did not go to these fairs with the expectation of finding prints, maps or books. I think things may have changed somewhat in the past dozen or so years and many print dealers now do these fairs regularly with a degree of success. This is especially true for the better, more upscale fairs such as the major New York antiques fairs. Map dealers have always tended to exhibit more at book fairs than at antiques fairs, except those that target the decorative market rather than the collector market. Serious map collectors visit the book fairs, not the antiques fairs.

129

F.J. Manasek

Book fairs are as diverse as the books one finds there. Almost every weekend one can find a book fair within a reasonable drive. Many of these fairs are sponsored by local booksellers' associations, others by promoters who organize fairs as a profit making venture. If one goes to local fairs often enough, either as a visitor or exhibitor, one rather quickly meets old friends. Many dealers have their books arranged in boxes, spines out. These boxes stack neatly on top of one another to form a bookcase-like display. When the dealers are setting up their displays at the fair, they dolly the boxes in, stack them up and turn on the lights. When they take down the fair, they reverse the process. In between fairs they store the book-filled boxes in cellar or garage, to wait for the next fair. As a result, the same books get exhibited a lot and we all get to recognize those that don't sell.

Local fairs are relatively cheap to do with booth rental often under a hundred dollars. Part-time dealers can afford to do these fairs, almost on a hobby basis, since they don't have to sell a lot of books to make expenses. Full time dealers will often exhibit at them in order to buy early. We can occasionally find unusual or underpriced books at the dealer preview, the time when exhibitors can buy from each other before the general public is admitted. Every exhibiting dealer looks at every other dealer's booth during this time. So, if there are a hundred dealers exhibiting, then each booth has been scouted by ninety-nine other dealers. What little remains is then offered to the general admission public when the fair opens.

Preview buying used to be very good. There was still enough material coming into the pipeline to warrant doing a show just for the preview buying. I know dealers who would travel from the west coast with a small number of books and rent a half-booth. Set up, for them, would involve spreading out the six or eight books they brought with them, a five minute job that left the rest of set-up time available for scouting. This practice has died out to a large extent as dealer inventories have become more and more picked over and fewer big-ticket items appear at these local fairs. At some of the major book fairs, such as the Antiquarian Booksellers' Association of America annual New York fair, the rental fee, now up to around three thousand dollars, is a bit too steep to warrant gambling on a few good pre-show buys. Nonetheless, I know of several dealers in England who do this still at the secondary London fairs. Here both volume and turnover is very large. Each fair usually has mostly fresh inventory and one never knows what may turn up.

Local fairs can be very downscale events. The grundge factor can be high and strange personalities prevail. I recall, in particular, one unusually dispiriting fair that seemed to specialize in dealers of Harlequin romance novels and Reader's Digest Condensed Books. The fair started out on a particularly difficult note. Hirsute Athena, her swarthy features glistening with dewdrops of sweat, stopped at the entrance to my booth. She had two huge boxes bulging with books, one under each arm. Their weight seemed to pull her down; somehow compress her and make her more stocky and squat than usual. Athena and her husband knew the used book trade very well and ran Jersey Turnpike Books, a large and prosperous secondhand book store just outside New York City. They loved to sell huge quantities of old books. Boxes of them; vans full of them; great piles of them. And they were very good at it. Athena spent much of her life buying these things at library sales and she always seemed to be weighted down with several boxes of them. Her strong features always scowled, her dungarees (to call them jeans would mock that very concept) were always dirty and her coarse hair always oily. I never had much to do with her except exchange a bit of chitchat now and then during book fair set-up time. Today, however, she was loaded for bear.

"What the hell are you doing at these shows?" she bellowed. "Look how you're dressed."

I looked down. Aha! I was wearing a blue button-down shirt and chinos. And a tie! Certainly grounds enough to engender a bellowing dislike in this loud, sebaceous individual. Good thing I wasn't wearing an ascot.

"You think you're too good for everyone else! I'll show you yet!" With that, she stomped off, book boxes bulging under the rippling muscles of her great arms, her soiled plaid shirt covering much of the greasy seat of her pants.

I never discovered Athena's true agenda, but I kept my back covered for the duration of that fair. I was told that Athena's husband had a nasty reputation. I also never figured out what set her off. Perhaps I had just ordered a gimlet in an Iron City Beer joint.

As opposed to the local book fairs, dealers from all over the world come to exhibit at the larger fairs. This provides a collector with the opportunity to see vast amounts of books, maps and manuscripts, indeed far more than would be possible to examine in any single city at any time. The fairs sponsored by the international dealer associations and their affiliates, such as the ABAA or the ABA are the flagship shows. Only members of the associations can exhibit here, and membership is still difficult to obtain. The fairs are large, professionally managed and attended well. It is to these shows that serious buyers and collectors come. Entrance fees are relatively steep, so the idly curious tend to stay away. At present, ABAA-sponsored fairs in the US are held in Boston, New York, Washington D.C., and on the West Coast where fairs alternate between Los Angeles and San Francisco. There are occasional fairs in Chicago, but this venue lacks an enthusiastic following and its future is uncertain.

The first Chicago ABAA fair was held, as I recall, in the late 70's. It was organized by the late Don Allen, a book dealer in Three Oaks Michigan. Don, and his wife Edith, worked very hard and managed to put together quite a nice fair. It was well attended and many of the exhibiting dealers told me privately that the fair had gone well for them. However, the bias against the midwest venue was so great that the fair was bad-mouthed almost universally. Don and

Uncommon Value

Edith were criticized vehemently, especially by those dealers who would never have even helped, and they both became bitter about the experience. Don quit the ABAA and always felt that he had been unfairly blamed for a difficult start-up fair. Nonetheless, even after many fairs have intervened between now and that first one, Chicago still has a poor reputation among the fair set and it remains to be seen if there will be future Chicago ABAA fairs.

The San Francisco Fair might be the world's largest. There are literally hundreds of exhibitors. I once figured a visitor could allocate six and a half minutes per booth if he came when the fair opened and wanted to visit each booth by closing time. San Francisco is an affluent city; people know what books are and they buy them. I always did well. However, in the past few years the fair has become so large that the quality declined. I also became unhappy with the venue. An unattractive building, it is located in a gloomy industrial part of town. There's no public transportation to it and although one can take taxicabs from downtown, it is difficult to get a taxi from the exhibition back to town. A couple of dealers got mugged a few years ago. I don't do this fair any more even though it still draws huge crowds. Living in Vermont, I'm not impressed by the world's biggest anything.

My favorite fair in which to exhibit is the New York ABAA fair, held in Manhattan each spring. The New York fair is the flagship American fair. I visited the first New York fair, I think it was in 1960 or '61 and have tried to go to every one since. There were several years I didn't make it, but it's an event to which I look forward. The fair is usually held in the armory just off Park Avenue. For a few years in the 80's it was in the Sheraton on the West Side. This was a difficult venue, it was hard to move in and out, and the space was crowded. It was a lovely place, though, and when all set up the red carpeted floors and the crystal chandeliers lent an air of elegance. Difficult and expensive to do, it attracted only the diehard dealers and we all did well. We brought our best items and the visitors responded. Moved back to the Armory, the fair grew in size and expense, but shrank in elegance.

We all have regular customers who make a point of visiting us at each fair and we often hold back special items for them to look at first. It's always a pleasure to see regulars at fairs.

Book fair exhibitors are all too familiar with the catalogue collectors. These are people who do not collect books, maps or anything other than catalogues listing these items. They visit each booth and take copies (sometimes handsfull of each.) of any literature or catalogues that we may provide. One sees these people staggering down the aisles, plastic shopping bags stuffed with catalogues, feverishly grabbing ever more. Some of them are overt about their collecting habit; others are furtive and skulk up to a display of catalogues and when they think you're not watching, grab a fistful, and scurry away before stuffing them into their bags. Held in amused contempt by most dealers, the catalogue collectors seem to think that the object of a fair is to grab as many freebies as possible. I think they are very angry people. I've occasionally asked them if they ever buy any books or if they just collect catalogues. In response, I've never gotten any answer other than glares or mutters or some kind of non-committal "Of course I have books." Invariably said with an angry voice.

Catalogues are expensive to produce. I illustrate our catalogues; some of them have forty or fifty photographic halftone illustrations. It can become quite expensive to keep the catalogue collectors supplied. I've told some to stay away from my catalogues. It doesn't really stop them, they hover around my booth like ankle biting curs just waiting to make off with a handful or two the moment my guard is down. Some dealers have begun charging for their catalogues, but giving free copies to legitimate patrons. It's surprising how the catalogue collectors avoid even the one dollar catalogues.

Uncommon Value

We also get the experts at fairs. These are the people who perhaps once in their lives saw a documentary film or read a Reader's Digest article on a topic and are now expert. Or the minor league academics who have to prove their expertise in musicology or whatever. I once had someone at the South Bend antiques fair tell me that all the medieval leaves I had on display were fakes. He knew, he said, because he had studied these in Rome, and besides, he was a Professor at Notre Dame. I believed the latter since he held most of the manuscripts right side up, but the guy obviously would have had trouble tying his own shoes. He, like others of his ilk, express his opinions in loud voices, probably with the intention of preventing anyone from buying.

The Chicago fairs were infested with a foul individual who talked loudly and incessantly. She told me she was "Dr. Surcia" and seemed to single me out for special attention."Well, Manachek," this spurious doctor would bellow, "how are you doing?" She was an expert on everything. I had been fortunate enough to acquire some wonderful Japanese calligraphy. Some fairly knowledgeable collectors were looking at it and had spread several pieces out on the table. At that moment, the ponderous Dr. Surcia thundered in.

"Well, Manachek, you still have that Chinese writing. I collect that, you know. All of it is fake you know." With that, she picked up a piece of my lovely Edo period calligraphy and tossed it aside contemptuously.

A little bit later, after I had concluded my sale, I had a quiet chat with Dr. Surcia and she never bothered me again. Carl Sandburg was quite correct when he labeled Chicago the "Hog Butcher to the world."

I was talking with a visitor to my booth at a Washington, D.C. fair. The visitor, who had inherited a small library, was looking for some advice and had asked me if I did appraisals. Suddenly, as though pouncing on some recent road kill for tonight's dinner, Jimmy Fistula thrust himself between me and my visitor. Jimmy Fistula was an ephemeral sort of person who had set himself up as a 'consultant' in rare books and maps. He was really a highfalutin' scout who would try to sell other dealers' items to his own customers. He also did appraisals.

"I do appraisals," said Jimmy Fistula, grabbing my visitor's arm and leading her out of my booth.

A little bit later, when I saw Fistula alone in another booth, I had a quiet chat with him and he never bothered me again. A couple of prominent local dealers later told me that Jimmy often does things like that. He's hard to embarrass.

A favorite trick of bargain hunters at book fairs is to wait until the fair is just shutting down. There is generally a feverish scramble at closing. Dealers want to get out as soon as possible and we all begin packing the moment the fair ends. Some bargain hunters, having located, during the fair, expensive items that they want, will wait until a minute before closing and then come around. Precisely at the moment the closing announcement comes over the P.A. system, they will make ludicrously low offers. I suppose it works in some cases, but not with me. However poor the fair might have been for me, I don't like being blackmailed. This is akin to the people who telephone a month or so after a catalogue has been issued to see what has remained unsold. They then try to make low offers on those items. I wonder if they do this at the local supermarket. My response is to take them off our mailing list.

There are wonderful fairs in Europe. Although it's a common American misconception that this is where the bargains are, I do attend them and buy and sell with some degree of success. The days are gone, however, when an American dealer could go to Europe and stock up with a year's inventory. These days it's more likely that we take a lot of inventory with us to sell there and hope that we can afford to buy some from our European colleagues.

I am particularly fond of the June fairs in London. There might be a dozen or more book and print fairs crammed into a one or two week period. It is literally impossible to attend all, so we each have our favorites. The madness usually kicks off with four days of fairs sponsored by the Provincial Book Fairs Association, or the PBFA.

The PBFA is a vibrant trade association that was founded some years ago in response to the exclusionary policies of the dowager queen of all booksellers associations, the Antiquarian Booksellers Association, or ABA. The ABA sponsors very expensive, posh book fairs that are probably the most exclusive and pricey anywhere. Booths of prominent dealers worldwide are filled with important works, or sometimes, average works priced beyond their importance. In recent years the ABA fair has fallen on hard times. The recession that caused so much financial suffering in London hurt this fair more than others. I think over the years prices here had become excessively high and despite good attendance, sales per exhibitor were declining. The venue provides elegant, but uncomfortable space and the crowds along with the sometimes stifling heat made fair attendance unpleasant at times. All this has served to decrease the viability of the ABA fair. In the 1993 fair, there were for the first time in my memory, unsold booths. Empty space at a London ABA fair! An unheard of disgrace.

The PBFA fairs, in contrast, are always filled, all the booths sold out and crowds of visitors buying. This might be a vindication of the reason for founding the PBFA, in response to the difficulty and expense of joining the ABA. While bottom end books are largely absent from the ABA fair (with booth rents at about £3000., one cannot afford to sell cheap books.) they are plentiful at the PBFA fairs. However, unlike the local book fairs in the US, where the material is largely low end, the PBFA fairs have a good percentage of higher end material as well. The fairs are well balanced, with something for everyone. If only they weren't so crowded.

London fair week is a frantic time, not only because of the overlapping fair schedule, but because we all want to visit as many dealers as possible, attend as many of the receptions as possible and see as many of our friends and colleagues as possible. Exhausting, sometimes profitable and always great fun. I've been doing it for years and although I've slowed down a bit and cut out some of the fairs, I wouldn't miss it. For as many years, after the fairs are over, I've always gone to Oxford, one of my favorite cities anywhere, to recuperate. Anne and I now generally spend a week in Oxford with the Old Parsonage Hotel as our base. This lovely old building has undergone a somewhat sensitive rehabilitation. I still have memories of it's prior incarnation when it was a little less designer-spiffy and not a whit less attractive. Indeed, the Old Parsonage was my base when, many years ago, I introduced Jared to the pleasures of Oxford. Nonetheless, it's still a great pleasure to sit in the courtyard in the warm June sun, savor the best martinis any English bartender ever made, and try to solve at least one of those confounded English crossword puzzles.

I rarely do any serious buying in Oxford, The big name shops in Oxford don't offer much. Oxford, being a tourist town, has generally high prices and an inventory that often was selected with the tourist in mind. A visit to the Magna Gallery on High Street is, however, rewarding and invariably pleasant. This is a nice little shop that sells maps and prints, mostly views of Oxford. The shop has appeared in at least several episodes of Inspector Morse. I also enjoy wandering the markets. The Jam Factory is an antiques marketplace near the train station. Here is where Valencia oranges were converted to marmalade when there still was an empire. Today the buildings are divided up into little stalls with dealers selling bits and pieces of old glass, estate jewelry and bric-a-brac. Mostly flea-market items, but occasionally one finds the better item. It's the hunt that matters.

Antiques markets are fun to visit and one never knows if a treasure lurks. It's sort of like buying lottery tickets, the chance of wining is minute, but it is zero if you don't have a ticket. That's what I tell myself when I get up in London's

Uncommon Value

pre-dawn to go to Bermondsey. London's Bermondsey Market occupies all of Bermondsey Square and spills over onto the adjacent streets. Surrounding buildings are extensions of the market and are filled with dealers and their goods. Located near Elephant and Castle, south of the Thames, the market opens before dawn each Friday and lasts until noon, when even the diehards fold. Jammed into tiny stalls, hundreds of pickers and dealers offer their goods. Bermondsey is a very ancient market and until recently the law of *market overt* applied to all transactions that took place within its confines. Ancient markets enjoyed this curious privilege which gave buyers at the market absolute title to all goods acquired there. Even stolen goods! Only recently was market overt abolished.

Bermondsey is a pro's market, certainly before 7:00 AM. In the winter months it's still dark when the market opens and a few enterprising dealers do a booming trade selling electric pocket torches. Everything from rubbish to handicrafts to extraordinarily valuable antiques passes through Bermondsey. I scout this market every time I'm in London. Hope springs eternal; rarely do I find anything suitable. I've gotten the occasional folding map here, but the market is not known for strength in paper or books.

An experience is probably the best way to describe the famous market at Portobello Road. Each Saturday, this market extends for several blocks along Portobello Road and intersecting streets. In tourist season the road becomes so jammed with people that it becomes difficult to walk, reminding me of another great market, Madrid's Rastro. Unlike the Rastro, Portobello has a greater emphasis on things old and one doesn't see the acres of new plastic merchandise that fills the Rastro.

Casual visitors to Portobello often are swept up by the color and character of the place and the people who sell there, often forgetting that the merchants earn their living at their stands. I recall some years ago seeing an American woman express obvious disappointment when the dealer would not bargain with her.

"You're supposed to!" she wailed. "The guidebook said you do."

"Listen, Miss, I don't have to do anything!"

Chapter 13

Turning the leaf

For some reason, I have trouble selling Holy Land maps. Some of these are extraordinarily beautiful as well as rare. An Ortelius Holy Land in original color showing the wanderings of Abraham is, in my mind, one of the most attractive maps around. All sorts of people come to me at fairs with the question I have learned to dread "Anything of the Holy Land?" Whatever I have is always dismissed with a wave of the hand and the now predictable "I have that," or "That is not for me." Over the years I must have had hundreds of these things and have placed precious few directly in private hands. I can't resist buying them because they indeed are attractive, rare, often expensive or all three. Also, enough people keep asking me for Holy Land maps that I keep trying to find the right formula. Other dealers don't have this problem and yet I cannot see any difference between their inventory of Holy Land maps and mine. Often, my prices are lower. I usually wind up putting them in an auction and am always pleasantly surprised. I usually get far more for them at auction than I would have realized in a private sale to a private client. This is not an unusual phenomenon, most people think that auction prices are 'wholesale' prices.

F.J. Manasek

I recall a particularly nice couple who visited me and asked about Holy Land maps. I showed them a beautiful 17th century Hornius/Jansson map. This is a very large map in 7 parts. Mine was exceptionally fine with early full hand color. A striking map. They liked it; they understood it, they could afford it. We talked about it, I discussed its history, I showed them references to it. They wanted it. They didn't buy it. Six months later, they were in Hanover again and came back to see me. It was nice to see them again, and we had a pleasant chat. They asked about 'their map' and I again showed it to them. They lusted after it. We talked price and it was not a matter of money. The map was not cheap, but it also wasn't one of the world's most expensive. I think it was around $900. They didn't even try to bargain on the price.

A few weeks later, I sent the map off to auction. It fetched well over a thousand dollars and I made a decent profit on it.

Yes, six months later the same couple returned for their biannual social call. They wanted to look at the map again. "Sorry, it's no longer here." I said.

"Oh dear, we wanted so much to see it."

"Were you interested in buying it?"

"No, I don't think so, but we wanted to look at it again. We wanted to see some things in it again." I was genuinely sorry to see them leave. I never saw them again. Manasek's Museum lost another visitor.

Shops such as mine are often confused with museums and libraries. I would get people coming in who were working on research projects, who had children who needed to look things up for their school reports, people who were curious about old things and parents who brought in their kids to touch and play with our rare books. "I'm looking for old maps showing eastern Pennsylvania in the 18th Century." might be an opening statement from a visitor. "Do you collect this area?" "No, I'm interested in towns and roads of that period. I used to have a house there and I want to see what it was like in colonial times."

These people had no intention of buying a map or a book, they simply wanted to look at one. I've no problem with that, but it is not the job description of our firm to provide such material to the public as a public service. Fiona was a saint and never gave these people short shrift, but I'm afraid I did.

"Do you have any books or maps on the West Indies?"

"Yes we do. In what sort of thing are you interested?"

"Well, I don't really know but my daughter has to do a report on Spanish colonialism in the West Indies and I was wondering if you had any maps."

"Yes, but they're quite expensive."

"Well, I don't want to buy them, I just want to get the information and I thought you could help me."

"Has she tried the library?"

"Huh?"

Time and again I've had individuals come in to my office and ask to use my inventory as reference materials or expect me to give them my time and then get very perplexed or very upset when I direct them to the library. I have come to wonder why we maintain libraries at public expense when most people don't seem to know what's in them or what they are for. In recent years the people of Hanover seem to have decided that the town library is a day care center and the library fills up in the afternoons with loutish, unruly kids that make it unusable as a library.

There is no doubt that some proprietors of used bookstores welcome this kind of interruption. Indeed, it is probably why they opened a bookstore. However, a small coterie of us do this for a living and run our businesses as businesses and it becomes impossibly expensive to spend a few hours a day entertaining idle prattle. Most of the serious dealers I know are plagued by this sort of thing. If it's a hobby for some, it must be for all. Some of these people who came simply to visit were genuinely nice individuals and I have no personal dislike of them, but it did my business no good whatsoever to expose myself to their visits.

A few years ago I began to consider seriously the possibility of shutting down the Hanover office and dealing privately. I talked with several of my friends in the trade who had done this and now deal out of their own homes, although some did keep very private offices.

There are pros and cons to both a shop and a home office and I explored them all. I finally decided to shut down the Hanover office on purely economic grounds. Rents had escalated to the point where I was paying about as much for my office in Hanover as I would have in Manhattan or Boston. And I had none of the advantages that come with those power locations. True, I had the personal advantage of living here in New England, but the business advantages did not warrant the rent. Further, the building I was in was in need of repair and I had suffered chronic water leaks from the heating system for the past two heating seasons. The bulk of my business was by mail with knowledgeable collectors, institutions and dealers all over the world. The clients who came to Hanover to browse my inventory could do that anywhere — I didn't need an expensive downtown office for that.

I am not alone in making this decision. In the past decade many dealers have decided to close their public premises for much the same reasons. Of course, there is always a bit of a stigma associated with working at home. Many people consider it the mark of a part time dealer. Part time dealers often carry lower-end maps and one is less likely to find better, i.e. scarcer items there. Beginning collectors also tend to shy away from coming to someone's house to look at maps or books. It can be a bit awkward if the distinction between a business visit and a social call is not made clear.

Uncommon Value

At about this same time Anne and I were looking for a larger house. We found a splendid house just a short walk from where we were living on the outskirts of Norwich, Vermont. Norwich is a small town with a population of about 3500. It is close to the Connecticut River just across from Hanover, New Hampshire.

The house that Anne and I bought came equipped with a wonderful post-and-beam two storey carriage house. A permit from the town was needed to move the business here. We had the carriage house remodeled; the large doors were removed and the interior was insulated and walled. We left as many of the beams exposed as was possible, put in a few big windows and a short while later, when the lease in Hanover was up, I moved the business and put away the sign. The new place has many advantages. It is completely separated from our house and visitors do not feel that they are intruding upon family quarters. I have, for the first time in many years, adequate space and, best of all, there is no walk-in. The place is very secluded, at the end of a private road, and not visible from the street. I screen potential visitors by telephone and discourage most. I don't think I'll ever have public space again. But then again...

Chapter 14

L'envoi

It's been a week since Anne and I have returned from our Christmas Holiday in Vienna. City of my father's birth, now home to my son. In a few weeks I go to Stuttgart. Book business, book gossip, old friends, good food and laughter. In the meantime, I work.

I have spent the day collating and savoring a wonderful 1589 Ortelius atlas. Full original color. It arrived last week and will go to my client in a few days. What a privilege to have owned this book, even for so short a time!

I look outside and see the early January snow shrouding the pine trees outside my office. Nature's Christo wrapping her own. The telephone hasn't rung, nor has howled the fax. James Granger, that old bookbreaking Oxford parson probably expressed it best. "I considered it to have been a stroke of good fortune to be able to retire early to independence, obscurity and content."